Finally! As the parents of two boys, this i [D1040631] for. And if you care deeply about your chilu about this book as we are. It's deeply grounded and incredibly practical. Don't miss out on this treasure trove of tested ideas you'll begin using immediately.

—DRS. LES AND LESLIE PARROTT, authors of #1 *New York Times* bestselling *The Parent You Want to Be*

Kara Powell and her team are doing some of the best work on student ministries and family life I know. Don't miss it!

—JOHN ORTBERG, Senior Pastor, Menlo Park Presbyterian Church

Have you ever wondered whether you have what it takes to be a spiritual leader for your child? This book not only affirms that you do but outlines practical steps, with stories of families who have paved the way with easy to follow ideas. A great guide for parents of all stages!

—SHERRY SURRATT, CEO and President, MOPS International

Kara Powell closes an important loop in the strategy to build authentic faith in the next generation. Now parents have a practical resource that will equip them to influence the spiritual direction of their own children. Like Kara's other books, this guide reflects a pragmatic approach seasoned with experience, which makes it a unique resource for every home.

—REGGIE JOINER, founder and CEO of Orange

For most families, faith tends to be more of an afterthought, something that easily slips away in the long days jam-packed with school, activities, and sports. This book helps moms and dads place faith back at the forefront of their lives with their kids. Your family will be deeply impacted by this profound and practical resource.

—MARGARET FEINBERG, author of *Wonderstruck* and *The Sacred Echo*

I implicitly trust Kara Powell (and the Fuller Youth Institute team) for excellent analysis and practical advice. I leverage it not only in my work with Q but also when I head home at night to engage with my children.

—GABE LYONS, founder of Q; author of *The Next Christians*

Kara Powell has done it again! She invites us to partake in a treasure chest of parenting wisdom. I have four post-high-school kids, and I'm still taking tips from her book. You'll love it. She offers ways to love your young person so that they will flourish.

— DAVE GIBBONS, founder of Newsong and Xealots.org; author
of *Xealots: Defying the Gravity of Normality*

This book invites busy and stressed parents to enter a whole new world of parenting. This research-based approach to family life and faith will change not only your kids but you too. Regardless of the ages of your kids, it's never too early or too late to point them to the God who sticks with us.

— MARK LABBERTON, PhD, President, Fuller Theological Seminary

Dr. Kara Powell serves up the extensive research of the Fuller Youth Institute with a wonderful self-deprecating sense of humor and an unusual honesty that obviously comes as much from how God continues to humble her as a parent as it does from her keen understanding of the many challenges that Christian parents and their children face today. This book is both profound and practical. I highly recommend it.

— REV. DR. KEN FONG, Senior Pastor, Evergreen Baptist Church
of LA (Rosemead, CA)

Scripture teaches us to "train a child in the way he should go, and when he is old he will not turn from it." Multiply that lesson by fifty, and you have an invaluable tool that every parent should read and have in their library. This book is just that, and I highly recommend it.

— ANGEL RUIZ, Field Ministry Vice President, Young Life

Sticky Faith, the idea that our kids can enjoy a relationship with God and the church that lasts a lifetime, is our number-one goal as Christian parents. Kara Powell and the FYI team have done a great job to provide this tool to help parents create an environment where kids can see and experience Jesus most clearly: in the lives of those who love him. Simple, doable, profound.

— CHAP CLARK, author of *Hurt 2.0: Inside the World of Today's
Teenagers*; Fuller Professor of Youth, Family, and Culture

the
stickyfaith
guide for
your family

Other Books Authored or Co-authored
by Kara Powell

Sticky Faith:
Everyday Ideas to Build Lasting Faith in Your Kids

Sticky Faith, Youth Worker Edition:
Practical Ideas to Nurture Long-Term Faith in Teenagers

Deep Justice in a Broken World:
Helping Your Kids Serve Others and Right the Wrongs around Them

Deep Justice Journeys:
Fifty Activities to Move from Mission Trips to Missional Living

Deep Ministry in a Shallow World:
Not-So-Secret Findings about Youth Ministry

the stickyfaith guide for your family

Over 100 Practical and Tested Ideas to Build Lasting Faith in Kids

Dr. Kara E. Powell

ZONDERVAN®

ZONDERVAN

The Sticky Faith Guide for Your Family
Copyright © 2014 by Kara Powell

This title is also available as a Zondervan ebook. Visit www.zondervan.com/ebooks.

Requests for information should be addressed to:

Zondervan, 3900 *Sparks Dr. SE, Grand Rapids, Michigan 49546*

Library of Congress Cataloging-in-Publication Data

Powell, Kara Eckmann, 1970 –
    The sticky faith guide for your family : over 100 practical and tested ideas to build lasting faith in kids / Dr. Kara E. Powell.
        pages cm
    Includes bibliographical references.
    ISBN 978-0-310-33897-0 (softcover)
    1. Christian education — Home training. 2. Christian education of children. 3. Christian education of teenagers. 4. Families — Religious life. I. Title.
BV1590.P69   2014
248.8'45 — dc23   2014011394

Published in association with the literary agency of WordServe Literary Group, Ltd., 10152 S. Knoll Circle, Highlands Ranch, CO 80130.

Cover photography: Adrea Scheidler
Interior illustration: iStockphoto®
Interior design: Beth Shagene

First Printing June 2014 / Printed in the United States of America

To Dave,
I love learning and living Sticky Faith with you and our kids.
You are the most Christlike man I know.

Contents

_____

Foreword

The statistics are staggering.

Today's generation of young people is not thrilled with the church and is leaving it—and its faith—behind.

Because of that reality, this is not just another book about the family. It's so much more important to the core of our faith both now and in the future. I am thrilled that we now have a hands-on book that brings together more than one hundred practical and tested ideas to build a lasting faith in kids.

While I grieve the young people who leave the faith, I take hope in this book's message that there is a much greater chance kids will stay connected to God if faith is modeled and talked about in the home. We know that preaching, lecturing, or ignoring faith issues in our families doesn't work. But developing faith-building rituals and conversations like the ones found in this book do work. That is why I encourage you to get started using the practical tools in this book to develop those faith conversations with your children.

If you work in the church, let me remind you that a majority of parents are timid about having conversations about faith. Your job is to offer valuable resources to them and to partner with them by handing them copies of this book. Parents know in their hearts these conversations are important; they just don't know how to have them.

When our own kids were younger, we started implementing "family nights" once a week. We chose fun food, had some kind of experience that was enjoyable, and then shared a few moments of faith conversations. I wish I could tell you every faith conversation was rewarding and life transforming. They weren't. But we believe those conversations along the road of life kept our kids grounded and our family focused on making our family what Kara calls "a hub of faith." We didn't have a book like this one, and that made it more complicated. But today, with great content like this, there really is no excuse not to try to create an environment at home in which your family's faith is nurtured and can flourish.

In every generation, God uses leaders and movements to create transformation in the church and in the lives of believers. I have said for years that Kara Powell is one of those leaders whom God has raised up for this generation. Kara leads the Sticky Faith movement with integrity, faithfulness, personal conviction, and brilliance like few people I know. Her academic credentials are impressive, but frankly, it's her life and lifestyle that make me want to learn everything I can from her. She lives out what she teaches. Why and how God chooses a leader like Billy Graham or Mother Teresa to lead movements and create renewal is for someone much smarter than me to figure out. But this I know: for centuries God has used individual leaders to spawn movements in which transformation happens. Kara is one of those leaders.

—JIM BURNS, PhD
President, HomeWord
Dana Point, California

Acknowledgments

"Go, team!"

If you were to eavesdrop on our Fuller Youth Institute (FYI) office conversations or peek at our email, you'd recognize that hardly a day goes by without one of us saying, "Go, team!" More than a mere slogan, those two words reflect our belief that it takes an enthusiastic, committed team to equip young people with the lifelong faith they need.

I am so grateful to God for the FYI staff, who pour their hearts and souls into all of our projects. One of my top ministry privileges is getting to dream, work, and learn alongside Brad Griffin, Jake Mulder, Haley Smith, Irene Cho, Matthew Schuler, Daniel Kim, Davin Tang, and Art Bamford.

The research in this book never would have happened without the vision and hard work of Dr. Cameron Lee, Dr. Krista Kubiak Crotty, Dr. Chap Clark, Dr. Scott Cormode, Dr. Cheryl Crawford, Dr. Erika Knuth, Dr. Chloe Teller, and Meredith Miller. A special thanks to Tim Galleher for spending his sabbatical interviewing amazing parents around the country and capturing their insights and stories.

We owe an enormous debt of gratitude to the parents and students we've interviewed over the years, who shared their experiences, hopes, and struggles. You have made me—and, I'm praying, will make every reader of this guide—a better parent and a more committed follower of Christ.

Along the way, a host of respected friends, parents, and grandparents reviewed the manuscript, giving pivotal suggestions. I'm grateful to Steve Argue, Roger and Lilli Bosch, Chris and Maggie Brandow, Dave and Robyn Coates, April Diaz, Lisette Fraser, Cindy Go, Amy Grable,

Jeff and Jenny Mattesich, Meredith Miller, Adam and Nancy Stiles, Angel Ruiz, and Albert Tate for their honest feedback.

The thoughtful editorial hand of Sandy Vander Zicht at Zondervan and the compelling vision of Greg Johnson at WordServe Literary Group have helped this Sticky Faith guide move from an idea to a reality.

FYI wouldn't exist without the visionary support of our advisory council, executive committee, and passionate supporters. We are especially grateful to those who have financially invested in our mission, including (but not limited to) Dale and Mary Andringa, Barbara Bere, Jim and Judy Bergman, Max and Esther De Pree, Brian and Linda Prinn, Sam and Betsy Reeves, Roy and Ruth Rogers, Mike and Valerie Volkema, Scott and Obaida Watt, Marion Wells, Dale and Cindy Wong, the Lilly Endowment, Inc., the Stewardship Foundation, the Tyndale House Foundation, and the Vermeer Charitable Foundation, Inc. A special thanks to my dear friend, mentor, and coach, Wally Hawley, whose belief in Sticky Faith fuels both me and our team.

I'm so grateful for the support of our extended family, especially my mom, who has pointed me and our kids toward God our entire lives.

Saving the best for last, I love being part of the Powell Team. Nathan, Krista, and Jessica, your honesty, wisdom, and love of fun inspire me every day. Dave, you are the partner God intended for me, and you far exceed my greatest dreams. Nothing feels real until I share it with you.

I can't imagine a better team!

Chapter 1

Why Does Your Family Need a Sticky Faith Guide?

Tennis balls.

I had to get tennis balls.

They were on the packing guide from the childbirth preparation class, so that meant one thing: they were essential.

You might be wondering, Why would a woman in labor need tennis balls? Our teacher suggested that while we were waiting for our baby to be born, we could put a tennis ball in a clean tube sock and use it as a massage tool.

I guess I needed a clean tube sock also.

The list from the childbirth class was fairly lengthy. Its specificity and breadth might have scared off other soon-to-be moms, but not me. My strategy was to follow the guide's every recommendation down to the last syllable.

In case you're wondering, yes, this was my first child.

So I needed chapstick.

And massage oil. Just in case my shoulders were aching and Dave's hands were too dry.

A deck of cards, a few magazines, and some music—in case we got bored.

VHS tapes (yes, I'm dating myself) of a few movies to pass the time during labor.

A roll of quarters for the pay phone. Mind you, both Dave and I had cell phones (we might have been using VCRs, but at least we had phones—albeit bulky ones), but the guidebook also recommended a handful of quarters, so I chased down some.

All of the above plus a few changes of clothes and my regular toiletries were in my carry-on suitcase three weeks ahead of time, carefully positioned by our front door for us to grab when it was time.

At 10:00 p.m. on a Tuesday, I went into labor. As I staggered to the car, Dave grabbed the suitcase, tossed it in the trunk, and made sure it made it to my hospital room for the big night.

Where it sat. Unopened. For my entire ten hours of labor.

We did open the suitcase the next day for my toothbrush. And a second time two days later so I could change from my shapeless hospital gown into shorts and a T-shirt for the ride home.

At least no one could accuse us of not following the hospital's guidebook for our son's birth.

Planning Ahead

I'd be surprised if any of you reading this book didn't plan ahead for your first few days with your child.

If you adopted your child, you planned the setup of their bedroom and made a few changes to your home. But more important, you thought about how to attach and bond with your new child. You likely had to work through intensive guidebooks and required training courses to become adoptive parents. Ahead of time, you tried to simplify your life and secure time off from work to make sure you would have the days and hours you wanted—and needed—to cocoon with your child.

If you or your spouse gave birth, you might not have been as extreme as I was. (In fact, I hope you weren't.) But you almost certainly chose the location. You likely strategized your route there. You probably even figured out how you were going to contact your friends and family, and maybe even who you were going to notify first.

I'm guessing that when it comes to planning for your first few hours with your child, you'd receive an A. (I myself was apparently trying for an A plus.)

But then something happens. Or rather, lots of somethings happen.

Our kids get older. We do too.

Our kids get busier. As do we.

Our kids seem to gain more energy. We seem to lose it.

If you're like me, you may have been proactive the first few days and even years of your kids' lives, but as your family's days become consumed by soccer practices and science tests, you become reactive. Instead of looking a few months or even years ahead, we consider ourselves lucky if we make it through the next few hours or days of our frenetic schedule.

At most, we devise plans for our children's education—both now and in the future. We think about schools they might want to attend and calculate the steps our kids (and we) need to take to boost their grades and extracurriculars. But that's often the only area of our family life where we have any long-term vision or goals.

For most families, faith tends to be more of an afterthought.

How Will a Sticky Faith Guide Help Your Family?

Let's get real: no part of parenting is easy. Whether we're responding to our fifteen-month-old's cries from the crib or our fifteen-year-old's texts from the mall, we're constantly improvising. Guessing. Hoping that what we're doing comes close to what's best for our kids.

Part of that is inevitable. Parenting will always be a messy (and often awkward) dance of art and science.

But what if there was research that removed at least some of the guesswork about what is best for our kids—both now and long-term? What if we could learn from proven tools and ideas that would help us create a plan for our families?

For some of us, following a plan is a joy. We are the type of folks who love making lists and identifying next steps.

For others of us, the term "plan" is a four-letter word. (Well, actually, it *is* a four-letter word for all of us, but you know what I mean.) We cringe at the thought of tying ourselves down to specific goals and tasks.

Regardless of whether you love or hate plans in other areas of your life, we at the Fuller Youth Institute hope you're willing to use this guide to map a spiritual course for your family.

Without a guide, without intentionality, your family is likely to drift. So is your kids' faith.

Multiple studies indicate that 40–50 percent of young people—like your kids—who graduate from a church or a youth group—probably a lot like your congregation or your kids' youth group—will leave their faith and the church after they head to college.[1]

To help that sink in, please take a moment to visualize a photograph of your kids and their Christian friends. Now imagine holding a red pen and drawing an X through almost 50 percent of their faces, because that many will fall away from the faith as young adults.[2]

As a mom, a leader, and a follower of Jesus, I'm not satisfied with that. I bet you aren't either.

As we at the Fuller Youth Institute have spent time with families who beat those odds—who are more successful than average at encouraging long-term faith—it's clear that those parents usually have a strategy that guides how they nourish their family's faith. It isn't that they are trying to control their children's future. Nor do they view following a guide as a foolproof guarantee for success. They hold the guide loosely, knowing that even their best-laid plans sometimes need to be tossed aside.

But these parents know that the things they care about—including their children's spiritual growth—stand a much better chance of becoming reality if they think in advance about what is important to them and how to make time for those priorities.

The mission of the Fuller Youth Institute is to equip teenagers with the lifelong faith they need. To find out more about how we leverage research into resources to help your family and church, and to access free Sticky Faith resources and subscribe to our free e-journal, visit *stickyfaith.org*.

These parents know that their kids' spiritual roots won't grow deep by accident. God is the ultimate gardener, but he often works through parents to prepare the soil, remove creeping weeds, and make sure kids have the spiritual nutrients they need to flourish.

Families who manage to beat the 50 percent statistic also helped our team confirm that it's never too early to start nurturing Sticky Faith. My husband and

I began implementing some of the ideas in this guide when our youngest was three years old. By starting when your kids are young, you can weave these research-based principles into the fiber of your family.

An important corollary is that it's also never too *late* to start nurturing Sticky Faith. During the course of our research and discussions with parents, we've heard countless stories of our loving God nudging a prodigal son or daughter back to their faith home. Sometimes the parent plays a visible role in this process.

More often, the parent plays a less visible role by praying—and praying hard—for their young-adult child to be overwhelmed with a sense of God's grace and mercy. Sometimes God uses challenges and crises to pull young people back to the faith; other times God works through a powerful experience of community or serving alongside others. Whatever the magnet, it's comforting to realize that faith development is a lifelong process for all of us, regardless of our age or faith leanings.

> Our son's legal problems started in middle school, but they exploded right after he graduated from high school. But during college the Lord drew him back into faith and the church. My son now is a junior-high leader at a church. I marvel at how God has brought him 180 degrees back to him, to serve other kids so that maybe he can help spare them the heartache that he went through.
>
> —Dawn

Findings and Ideas: A Dynamic Duo

I'm a researcher who's married to an engineer. To say that our family values data is an enormous understatement. Dave and I never met a spreadsheet we didn't like.

As much as I applaud data, I cheer even more enthusiastically when data is translated into practical resources. It's the application of data that guides you and me toward a strategy that fits our unique parenting styles. It's the pairing of research with proven ideas that empowers families to walk forward in their pursuit of relationship with Jesus and each other.

In every chapter of this book, you'll get a front row seat to research-derived findings that can help you develop lasting faith as a family. While we could have deluged you with statistics and trends, we ruthlessly mined the data to unearth the handful of insights essential to your family's strategy.

We call them "findings" because they have emerged from valid and reliable research. Yet we need to be clear in the early pages of this guide that there is no formula for building Sticky Faith. Much of the research we share is correlational in nature—meaning that the more families adopt certain practices, the more their kids *tend* to have lasting faith. Other findings have grown out of qualitative research, where we've interviewed fifty parents like you and looked for common practices. So while it makes sense to adopt those practices, there is no golden blueprint that will yield unwavering faith.

After all, we try hard as parents, but ultimately it's the Holy Spirit's job to build deep faith in our kids. (I hope you sighed in relief after you read that sentence. I did after I wrote it.) Because God is the one who ultimately sticks with us and our kids, we can trust him to walk with our families no matter what we face.

After we run through some foundational findings in each chapter, ideas from families we've studied will take the field. Like you and me, these parents are regular folks who love their kids and want the best for them. They are not perfect, but they have raced, walked, and sometimes stumbled toward being a faith-pursuing family. Along the way, they've picked up some bumps and bruises, as well as a lot of wisdom that can help us.

Some of these ideas are blatantly connected to prayer and Scripture and feel very "spiritual." Others are more tied to meals or miniature golf and feel more "fun" or "relational." The reality is that the family bonding during car trips and card games is indeed very spiritual. Similarly, exchanging prayer requests in your family and adopting a family Bible verse are activities that tighten your family's relationships with each other. So we present both relational and spiritual ideas, praying that the Holy Spirit will help you sort out which hold the most promise for your family's road map.

No longer do the finest faith-building ideas need to remain hidden from view, practiced privately by scattered families. They are now gathered in your hand, on your coffee table, and across your screen.

The Sources for the
Sticky Findings and Ideas

Most of the findings and ideas to help your family develop lasting faith come from three sources. The first data stream flowing through this guide is six years of research we at the Fuller Youth Institute conducted with more than five hundred youth group graduates from churches nationwide. Our team's goal was to follow these students during their first three years of college to discover the steps that churches and families could take to help set young people on a trajectory of lasting faith.

As we have shared the results of that study with parents nationwide through presentations and our first book, *Sticky Faith*, they have begged us for more practical ideas, ideas we knew we could best glean from families themselves. So the second data stream running through this guide is fifty interviews the Fuller Youth Institute team conducted during 2012–13 with parents across the United States. Nominated by church leaders, these parents are of different geographical regions and denominations, various marital situations (while the majority are married, some are single parents, and others are remarried), and diverse ages and ethnicities.[3] What they share is a commitment to deepen their kids' faith, and a recognized effectiveness in doing so. These parents are far from flawless, but they are willing to share what seems to have helped their kids keep the faith.[4] To our delight, their experiences both confirmed what we had learned from our first data stream of five hundred young people and opened our eyes to new tributaries of insights and ideas that help families build enduring faith.

For more information about the research methodologies we followed as we interviewed five hundred youth group graduates and fifty parents, see appendixes 1 and 2.

While these two studies yielded a treasure trove of insights, we also appreciate the studies conducted every day by fellow researchers around the country, and these studies are the third and final stream contributing to this guide. Our team extensively reviewed the top research on faith development and family dynamics to showcase the best for you.

This guide thus brings to your kitchen table the top voices in the country on Sticky Faith families. You get to pull up a seat also.

These three streams of research (our two studies and our review of other research) form a river that flows through my own parenting. Every day, my husband and I parent differently—and better—because of the findings and ideas we've garnered from other families.

In some ways, the findings comprise the "head" of Sticky Faith families, while the ideas are the beating "heart." Findings without ideas lead to irrelevant rationalism. Ideas without findings degenerate into empty emotionalism. But together, they allow you to understand not only *why* your family needs to make some strategic changes but also *how* to get there.

How Is This Book Different from Sticky Faith?

What began as a study of five hundred young people became the first Sticky Faith book, *Sticky Faith*.

That first book, as well as additional resources for families and churches, has become a Sticky Faith movement, a divinely fueled coalition of leaders and parents from all fifty of the United States and from sixty other nations committed to loving and serving young people differently.

Because parents who have joined the movement have asked us for even more research-based ideas, we developed this book. While most of the findings are brand-new, since not everyone who reads this book will have read the first Sticky Faith book, a handful of pages in this book review material presented in that first book. Because every single idea is new, and since we have emphasized ideas even more in this book than in previous resources, fans of *Sticky Faith* will have plenty of new tips and tricks to try at home.

How Your Family Can Get the Most out of This Guide

When we sifted through the most eye-opening findings and ideas, eleven themes emerged, each of which is described in its own chapter.

As you work your way through the findings and ideas in each theme, we're hoping you're going to want to be a better parent.

But if you're like me, these insights may cause your "I've already failed as a parent" dial to click a few extra notches higher.

Or maybe these ideas will add a few more pounds to your "I'm not as good as other parents" scale.

I remember the Monday I conducted five consecutive one-hour interviews with Sticky Faith parents. By the end, I could barely stand myself as a parent. I felt more insecure than inspired. The stories and ideas I heard felt more like a punch in the gut than a shot in the arm.

One parent was amazing at involving his kids in serving others. Another excelled at making memories. Still another was a genius at making their home the go-to place for their kids' friends.

I felt like a munchkin surrounded by parenting giants.

You might feel the same as you flip through this guide.

Peaks and Pits

The problem is that we compare the *worst* of what we know about ourselves with the *best* of what we have heard from other parents. On my Monday marathon of interviews, I had temporarily forgotten two truths: first, that even these "successful" parents experience failure after failure. The great ideas that we're sharing in this guide often emerged out of a messy process in which parents' ideas fell flat. Like the great baseball hero Babe Ruth, the parents we are profiling hit a lot of home runs, but they also strike out a lot.

While the majority of this book focuses on great ideas, we know you will be encouraged by hearing about not just parental triumphs but also parental tragedies. We've sprinkled throughout this guide quotes of parents and students describing their family peaks and pits (to quote one of those parents). We've also added a dozen sidebars with research-based tips to tackle your toughest "what if" questions. We hope these sidebars give you a courtside view of families who've been playing the parenting game longer than you. They are banged up, but they are savoring the joy of continuing to point their families toward Jesus.

Not only that, but we've devoted an entire chapter to how to respond to mistakes, both your kids' mistakes and your own. On the journey to Sticky Faith, our mistakes can actually be a gas pedal toward our family's faith development, if we handle them wisely.

Pick and Choose

The second truth that I had forgotten is that no one family is capable of embracing every great parenting strategy.

Every family picks and chooses.

You too have to pick and choose what's best for your family.

I recommend that on your first time through this guide, you choose no more than five ideas to try. Five (or fewer) ideas are doable. More than that and you'll likely try to accomplish too much too quickly. As any runner knows, the journey of a marathon starts with the first few steps.

Note that I wrote "your first time through this guide." We've designed this guide to be like a recipe book or a playbook for your favorite sport. We hope you return to it again and again, sometimes skimming from the first page to the last, and other times doing a deep dive into the one chapter most vital to your family in that season.

To help your family best use this Sticky Faith guide, we are providing the following tools and suggestions.

1. *At the end of each idea*, we give you a chance to quickly reflect on how, if at all, this idea would guide your family toward long-term faith.

2. *At the end of every chapter*, we invite you to take a short quiz to rank how your family aligns with the findings and to reflect on which ideas might be most beneficial for your family. If you are reading this guide with friends or your small group, those questions are a great springboard for face-to-face discussions.

3. *At the end of the guide*, we provide a final chapter to help you flip through the quizzes at the end of each chapter and design a strategy to implement your five favorite Sticky Faith ideas.

4. *The day you finish the guide*, we encourage you to post your five favorite ideas in a public place—such as on your bathroom

mirror or on your kitchen whiteboard—or in your favorite note-taking app.

5. *The week you finish the guide*, we hope you pick up the phone and call or meet face-to-face with a friend who can hold you accountable for making headway on those five ideas. Even if they haven't read the guide yet, they can still periodically ask you how you are doing and strategize with you how to move forward at a pace that fits your family.

   Of course, we hope you're engaged with a congregation or community of fellow believers. If appropriate, share your five favorite ideas with your children's pastor, youth pastor, or small group leader. In their interactions with your children, they can help water the seeds that you are planting at home.

6. *A month or two after you finish this guide*, we invite you to evaluate your top five ideas list, noting which ideas seem to be working, which should be tweaked, and which should be replaced by new ideas that would better fit your family. Often the parents we interviewed found they had to do several experiments before landing on what worked best for their families. If you find yourself discouraged or in need of fresh ideas, you'll probably benefit from rereading a few chapters to refresh your enthusiasm and vision for what God wants to do in and through your family.

Suzanne's Story

My interest in developing a Sticky Faith family myself—and helping you do likewise—is partially fueled by Suzanne. For Suzanne and her three sons, the hopeful and practical message of this Sticky Faith guide came at just the right time. Suzanne had always believed in one of our core research-based practices, which we share in chapter 6: she surrounded her kids with a team of caring adults. But when, at a weekend family camp, Suzanne heard some of the facts and ideas behind that practice, she finally understood both why a team of invested adults is so important and how to build it.

Over the next few months, Suzanne and her husband asked her boys which adults they'd like to get to know better. Next Suzanne and her husband invited those adults to care for their boys. Across the board, those adults felt honored by the invitation to join the web of adults that surrounds each boy.

The need for a caring team of adults climaxed a year later when Suzanne was diagnosed with colon cancer. Convinced of the importance of encircling her sons with support, Suzanne continues to enlist men and women to come alongside her three boys as she battles cancer. If the Lord chooses not to heal Suzanne physically, these adults will likely walk with her sons for years to come.

We could stop Suzanne's story there and be inspired, but the story continues.

Suzanne isn't just building long-term faith in her own sons. On days she is physically able, she also invites neighborhood kids into her home so that those kids and their parents can get glimpses of a family transformed by Christ. Motivated by the thought of the role she can play in other kids' faith, Suzanne shares, "I'm excited to see how God is going to work through our family to reach the families in our neighborhood."

Not only has Suzanne developed a pathway for her own family; she's become part of other families' faith journeys. Just like you, she is part of the Sticky Faith movement rolling forward and changing the world one kid at a time.

As you join this growing team of parents, the last thing you need is a book that showers you with feelings of guilt for all you're not doing.

The first thing you need is a book that plants seeds of hope and strategy, enabling you to prayerfully point your family toward Jesus.

We hope and pray this guide is that first thing.

Chapter 2

You Get What You Are
Modeling Sticky Faith

"I'm Kah-wa Powell."

What our youngest child, Jessica, lacked in pronunciation of the letter *r*, she made up for in her gusto for pretending to be me. Every day for two months, she plunged into my bedroom closet, grabbed as many items as her five-year-old fists could carry, and then wore them over her own clothing. Her favorite items were my black leather boots, an orange blouse, a turquoise scarf (trust me, it isn't as eighties as it sounds), a gold linen dinner jacket (okay, that is as eighties as it sounds), and a wool hat.

Regardless of how you evaluate her fashion sense, if you saw her walk around our house, you'd see that she had a sixth sense for imitating me. Stumbling awkwardly in boots that were twice the size of her feet, she'd grab my briefcase on wheels and stride across our wood floors, proclaiming to all other family members, "I'm Kah-wa Powell."

It was even more adorable than it sounds.

It got less adorable when Jessica started imitating facets of my parenting. She'd stand in our living room, wag her finger at an invisible daughter sitting on our navy blue couch, and sternly warn, "Jessica, you need a better attitude."

Imaginary Jessica didn't seem to improve. My daughter's remedy? More wagging of the finger, mixed with, "Jessica, go to your room."

Sometimes she'd invite friends to join in the dress-up play. Jessica was always "Kah-wa Powell," and the friend was usually talked into being "Jessica." What did "Kah-wa" and "Jessica" do together? Play cards? Sit and read? Color at the kitchen table?

Nope. "Jessica" usually spent most of her time on the couch, receiving a lecture from "Kah-wa Powell" about what she had done wrong.

One Friday afternoon, another mom whose daughter had been at our house for the afternoon was invited to watch a "play" that the two five-year-olds had created. In this play, there were no fairies, doggies, or princesses. The "story" (if you've watched your five-year-old child's plays, you know that the quotes are warranted) revolved around my black-booted, briefcase-wheeling daughter playing me and giving her "daughter" a grim lecture.

The other mom and I laughed (somewhat awkwardly) at my daughter's portrayal of me. But long after the other family walked down our driveway, one question sat on the front steps of my heart: *Is that my daughter's primary picture of me?*

Jessica mirrored to me a posture and a tone of voice that was everything I didn't want to be as a mom. As she acted out her version of how I corrected her, I knew I was the one who needed correcting.

Sticky Findings

1   We Will Get What We Are

After studying the faith development of more than three thousand young people nationwide from Protestant, Roman Catholic, Jewish, and Mormon families, Christian Smith and his team concluded, "The best general rule of thumb that parents might use to reckon their children's most likely religious outcomes is this: 'We'll get what we are.'"[1] As important as this guide's other ten factors are in building Sticky Faith families, the reality is that in general, the primary influence in a child's faith trajectory is his or her parents.

As with all findings in this guide, please take this with a grain of salt. Or even a moun-

> *The most important social influence in shaping young people's religious lives is the religious life modeled and taught to them by their parents.*
>
> —Christian Smith and Melissa Lundquist Denton (Smith and Denton, *Soul Searching*, 56)

tain of grains of salt. You might have a very different faith journey than your parents'. You might have multiple kids who are choosing different faith paths themselves.

While there is no foolproof formula, in integrity as a researcher I need to be clear: your strategy for developing a Sticky Faith family starts by assessing the vibrancy of your own faith.

2   We Will Get What Our Kids Think We Are

Having grasped the importance of our faith example, we can move to a more nuanced—and accurate—understanding of the power of our beliefs and behaviors. As important as our faith lives are in influencing our kids, multiple studies of teenagers indicate that more important than what parents believe is what teenagers *perceive* they believe.[2]

When I was a high school student, our youth pastor decided to make the focus of one of our Wednesday night meetings this question: If you were on trial for being a Christian, would there be enough evidence to convict you?

To my surprise (and dismay), I was one of the three students picked to be on trial. Friends of mine from youth group then gave testimonies about both my character and my behaviors. I remember sitting on a gray plastic chair in the front of our youth room, palms

> We can't out-teach what you teach at home. We're not that good.
>
> —Dr. David Fraze, Director of Student Ministries, Richland Hills Church of Christ

sweating and heart pounding, wondering if there was going to be enough evidence to convict me.

There was. In my opinion, barely.

Because that sort of mock trial can easily become emotionally manipulative and guilt producing, I don't recommend trying this at your home church. But given the research on Sticky Faith families, I hope you reflect on this question: If I were on trial for being a Christian, what evidence could my kids offer to convict me?

3   *There Are Many Ways to Build and Model Sticky Faith in Front of Your Kids*

As we interviewed parents who had developed enduring faith in their kids, one theme emerged: they made the cultivation of their own faith a priority.

While that was a nearly universal goal, there were no universal steps parents took to make that goal a reality. Each parent seems to find their own channel to stay in tune with Jesus.

Some hold traditional "quiet times," often in the morning before children are looking for breakfasts and backpacks.

Others prefer to journal in the evenings while kids are sleeping or studying.

Some like to sit.

Others feel closer to God while moving—while jogging, walking, gardening, or even driving.

Some need quiet.

Others prefer the stimulation of a good sermon or great worship music, or even the background noise of a coffee house or the morning bus commute.

The length, location, and posture of parents' time with God vary. What is constant is their recognition that regular (generally daily) time with God needs to be a priority in their schedules.

4   *Our Marriages Shape Our Kids' Faith*

While not as formative as our relationship with God, the quality of our marriages also affects our family's faith trajectories. A nationwide study of more than 1,100 adults examining the effects of family of origin on church involvement found a modest association between the marital happiness of a person's parents and that person's religious involvement. In other words, people whose parents had marriages that were more life-giving were also more likely to attend and be involved with a faith community.[3]

While the nature of our marriages seems to be a factor in our kids' faith development, it's important to note that the effect is mild. So if you are a single parent or walking through a challenging marriage season, take heart. With some prayerful planning, the relational glue of your extended family and the faith community can help compensate for what's missing at home. (Chapter 6 is wholly devoted to this.)

Sticky Ideas

Same Time, Same Place

Of the parents we interviewed, the majority were most successful in carving out time with the Lord when they found a consistent rhythm.

Same time.

Same place.

Every day.

Or at least most days.

The twenty minutes every morning before their kids appear in the living room.

The fifteen-minute commute to work each day after dropping off their kids at school.

The twenty-minute walk after dinner to get some fresh air.

The ten minutes every night in bed before they turn out the light.

Even if it wasn't daily, it was consistent. One busy executive found it challenging to carve out time with the Lord on weekdays, so he spent an hour reading the Bible and praying first thing every Saturday morning. While he wished he spent such focused time with God more frequently, he rarely missed his Saturday routine.

Personally, I double my chances of working out if I plan the day before when I'll make it to the gym. I triple those chances if I put on workout clothes as soon as I get out of bed.

For many Sticky Faith parents, identifying a consistent time and place similarly increases the likelihood of developing their spiritual muscles.

Your Family

- What is your best daily, or regular, opportunity to connect with the Lord?
- Why do you think that connection is so powerful?
- What would need to change in your schedule to make that time a greater priority?
- What could you do the day before (whether it be to get the kids' lunches ready or to check email one last time before going to bed so it's not as stacked up in the morning) that would help you stay more consistent?

What if I'm not the Christian I want my kids to be?

If you feel that way, you and I should start a club. It would be a very large club.

If you are in touch with your sin, you realize that while Jesus has already forgiven you and granted you eternal salvation, you are not yet fully transformed into his image (this is often referred to by theologians as the "already/not yet" tension).

I'd be more worried about you if you were telling me that you are the Christian you want your kids to be. I would wonder if you need a deeper whiff of the cesspool of sin from which God continues to cleanse and redeem us.

Having said that, if you're asking the question, you might need to evaluate the direction and pace of your spiritual growth. One of my favorite quotes by

Dallas Willard is, "We are becoming who we will be forever."* Our daily decisions, relationships, and habits have the potential to mold us into either a self-centered lump of clay or the Christ-centered vessel that God intends.

So what one (let's choose just one to keep it manageable) regular practice might God use to help transform you into the person he wants you to be? Could it be the ongoing study of Scripture? Or maybe time in prayer, listening for God's specific messages for you? Perhaps a weekly Sabbath? Or possibly community with other believers who know the song in your heart and sing it to you when your memory fails?

If you're not sure, ask God to show you where to start. Write down what you want to try and schedule it on your calendar. If you skip a day (or two or five), don't panic. Celebrate the growth you see in yourself. Even if some months you take three steps forward and two steps back, you're still one step closer to the parent and disciple God has created you to be.

* Dallas Willard, *The Divine Conspiracy* (San Francisco: HarperCollins, 1998), 11.

 ## A Running Conversation with Jesus

While regularly scheduling time to pray, read Scripture, and meditate is hard, I find a second practice of some dedicated parents even more challenging. And convicting.

It's not as pervasive a theme as the power of regular times with the Lord, but several parents we interviewed found great spiritual strength by maintaining a regular conversation with Jesus. They would comment that they "pray all the time" and maintain a "regular conversation with Jesus" in the midst of work and family responsibilities.

As one parent described, "Whatever happens during my day, I keep my conversation going with the Lord."

Some parents find that praying some or all of the "daily office" of fixed-hour prayer (common in Anglican and Roman Catholic traditions) helps pace their day with "God pauses." Whether on their smartphone or in a book, these excerpts from Scripture and the prayers of others can be a catalyst for ongoing conversation with God.

In talking with these parents, I don't sense that they do this because it's merely a good idea. To them, it's like a spiritual oxygen mask, helping them stay calm and breathe when they hit turbulence.

Your Family

- In what times of your work and personal life are you most likely to turn to prayer?

- What difference would it make in your life and family if you were even more likely to do so?

A Day a Quarter

Cliff, a dad of two teenagers, has found he connects with God best when he isn't rushed or preoccupied with his next meeting. So Cliff sets aside a day each quarter as his time away with God. Grabbing his Bible, a few books, and a lunch, he heads to a nearby park, lake, restaurant, or friend's vacant house for the day. (Cliff lives in Minnesota, so the time of year makes a big difference in where he holes up.) These quarterly days are Cliff's lifeline, enabling him for the next three months to be the disciple, leader, husband, and dad that he longs to be.

Your Family

- Maybe an entire day isn't feasible for you, but what would be? A half day? Two hours?
- What could you do during that time that would feed your soul?

 ## Praying with Your Calendar

If your calendar seems too full for any of these ideas, perhaps prayer itself is the solution. Abigail, a mom with college-age sons, has found that taking time to pray actually gives her more time to pray. How does that time-math work?

When Abigail prays with her calendar in front of her, the Lord often gives her a sense of what is most important to him and to her family. As a result, she inevitably eliminates some of the items crowding her to-do list. Prayer helps Abigail become more able to identify those tasks that can wait or, even better, don't need to be done at all.

Your Family

- When in the past have you felt God guiding you on how to spend your time?
- If you were to pray through your calendar, what do you think the Lord might nudge you to cut?

- What's keeping you from eliminating those time commitments right now?
- How might praying with your calendar help you face the necessary tasks of your day with more faithfulness?

Community as a Portal for Spiritual Growth

Many parents we interviewed mentioned the catalyzing role of others in their own spiritual growth—particularly close friends, mentors, and fellow members of Bible studies or small groups. When parents' frustration or fatigue makes them blind to God's vision for their lives or families, it's often others who show them the way.

As with other ideas that further spiritual growth, these relationships almost always take planning. One single parent makes double dinner every Wednesday night, carefully placing extra plates in the refrigerator with her kids' names on them, so she can make it to her Thursday night small group. That additional work is worth the payoff that comes from spiritually rubbing shoulders with other women every week.

Your Family

- When you become blind to God's vision for your life or family, who points you in the right direction?
- Who else could help you grow spiritually?
- How can you get the time you need with these folks to be sharpened spiritually and personally?

Feeling a bit spiritually inadequate as you read about these amazing parents? You're not alone. Keep in mind that we want you to choose only *five* ideas throughout the entire book, so please pace yourself. If you're feeling guilty for all you aren't doing as a parent and follower of Jesus, we'll tackle how to handle mistakes (both ours and our kids') in chapter 3.

A Bath Every Night for Thirty Years

Daily walks.

Weekly date nights.

Annual anniversary weekends.

Those were the ideas we expected to hear—and did hear—from husbands and wives sharing their secrets for nurturing their marriages.

I wish I had been in a Bible study when my kids were teenagers. It would have been helpful for me and my husband to have that support from peers who were walking the same life journey. Otherwise you feel like you're doing this all by yourself. When our daughter came home and looked at us like we couldn't do anything right—not even breathe—being with others in a small group would have helped us feel less alone.

—Laura

In the midst of our interviews, perhaps the most unique idea we heard was from a couple who have been married for more than thirty years. Every night before bed, Don and Debbie go into their master bathroom and take turns taking a bath. It's their thirty minutes to decompress, debrief their days, and discuss their kids (and now grandkids).

Yes, every night. For thirty years.

As Don summarized, "We always know at the end of the day that we have that time to connect."

Your Family

- What could you do every day—or most days—that would be your own special way of connecting with your spouse?

Date Night Kid Swap

Some parents have extended family nearby who are quick and eager (maybe at times too eager) to babysit. It's usually a great win-win-win. Grandma and Grandpa get time with their grandkids. You and your spouse get to have an uninterrupted meal or actually watch a whole movie in one sitting. And your kids get extra sugar and electronics time.

Those parents who don't have the blessing of local extended family often struggle with scheduling date nights. Finding a babysitter is yet one more task to do. Funding that babysitter is yet one more bill to pay.

Rick and Monica have solved this dilemma by arranging a "date night swap" with another family. One Wednesday night, Rick and Monica's kids go to the other family's house for a meal and a few hours of hang-out time. Two weeks later, the kids from the other family come to Rick and Monica's house so the other couple can have a dinner date.

Not only is it cheap and easy; it is scheduled. Rick admits, "Even when my wife and I are busy, or feeling a bit distant from each other and don't feel like going out to dinner together, we have date nights built into our calendar. Our arrangement with the other family forces us to do it, and we are always glad we do."

Your Family

- Given your season of life, what frequency of date nights makes sense?

- If childcare is an issue, is there another family you could exchange kids with every two to four weeks? Your taking initiative with the other family would likely be a blessing to them also.

- If you're a single parent, who are the trusted friends who most energize and support you? How could you set a consistent rhythm for spending time with them without your kids?

 ## The Power of a Purple Pen

It's no secret that strong communication lies at the heart of strong marriages. What is less recognized is the power of communicating in words and actions that are most meaningful to your spouse.

After being married for eighteen years, Bill and Carolyn started teaching a premarital class. During this time, they came across Dr. Gary Chapman's teaching that each person (including you and your spouse) has their own "love language." Your love language is the way you prefer to give (and, often more important, receive) tangible signs of love from the people who are important to you.[4] Dr. Chapman has identified five love languages:

- Words of affirmation
- Acts of service
- Receiving gifts
- Quality time
- Physical touch

According to Bill, "Carolyn's love language is receiving gifts. I've found I don't have to give her a five-hundred-dollar piece of jewelry to speak her love language. Just bringing home a pen from a hotel that's her favorite shade of purple means the world to her."

Although Carolyn might prefer the jewelry.

Your Family

- What would you guess is your spouse's love language? (Or even better, ask your spouse so it's not a guess.)
- How can you "speak your spouse's love language" in caring actions or words this week?

Our Family's Steps toward Sticky Faith

Take a few moments on your own, or with your spouse, your friends, or your small group, to reflect on some potential next steps toward Sticky Faith.

Sticky Findings

On a scale of 1 to 5 (with 1 being "we stink at this" and 5 being "we rock at this"), rate your family on the research findings presented in this chapter.

1| I myself have the vibrant faith I hope my kids will have as adults.

① ② ③ ④ ⑤

2| My kids observe me living out my faith in our home and community.

① ② ③ ④ ⑤

3| I make the cultivation of my faith a priority in my schedule.

① ② ③ ④ ⑤

4| I feel supported and enriched by quality friendships and/or my marriage.

① ② ③ ④ ⑤

Sticky Ideas

1| What are you already doing that is helping you model faith in front of your kids?

2| In what ways are you and your children already benefiting from a supportive marriage or friendships?

3| Given your ranking of the findings in the previous section, as well as the ideas you've read in this chapter, what one or two changes might you want to make in your family?

4| What can you do in the next few weeks or month to move toward these changes?

Handling Mistakes
Showing Sticky Forgiveness

Perhaps your children have the same continuum of crying as ours.

On one end of the continuum is fake tears.

Next comes "I'm tired" crying.

Followed by "I think you won't punish me if I cry" tears.

Then "I'm mad or sad or scared and need you" tears.

And finally "the world is ending and I can't stop crying" waterworks.

One Tuesday morning, Krista's tears pegged the last. Our then eight-year-old walked into our bedroom in full-blown, wet-faced panic.

Krista has always loved to read. Her nightstand is invariably covered with books. She also loves to have a glass of water at night. That morning, Krista learned the hard way that books and water don't mix well.

"Mom, water was spilled on a book." (I'm regularly struck by how our kids use the passive voice when they make mistakes. It wasn't that Krista spilled the water; it was that the cup somehow mischievously decided to tip itself over and spill its contents.)

She managed to catch her breath in the midst of her tears. "It's a library book. I don't want to tell the school librarian what happened. I don't want to have to tell Mrs. Heidenreich." (I'm not making that up; that's actually the school librarian's name.)

I hugged my weeping daughter. Together we walked to our laundry room, spread the sopping book on towels, and aimed a hair dryer toward its soggy pages. I wasn't sure that our paper patient would fully recover, but spreading the book over towels seemed to calm my daughter. By the time we jumped in our van and headed to school, Krista was back to her normal self.

Until we pulled into the school's car line. As Nathan and Jessica grabbed their backpacks and slid out of our van, Krista panicked. "Mom, my stomach hurts. I can't go to school." More tears, this time of the "I'm scared and need you" variety.

Allowing Krista to stay in the car, I drove across the street and into the school's parking lot. Unbuckling my seatbelt and turning to face her in the back seat, I wondered aloud, "Krista, since you didn't mention your upset stomach until we got to school, perhaps what's happening is you're scared about the library book."

I don't have a medical degree, but I do know our daughter.

I continued, "Sometimes when I'm nervous about something, my stomach gets upset. Do you think that's what's happening?"

Nods from the back seat.

I make so many errors as a parent. I regularly say the wrong thing, or say the right things in the wrong tone of voice. But this was one of those times when the Holy Spirit helped me. I knew exactly what I needed to say to Krista.

It was six words. Six words that I now share with every young person I can. Six words that I hope become a mantra in your family, as they have in ours.

The six words I told Krista are, "Jesus is bigger than any mistake."

I added, "Krista, if Jesus can't handle a wet library book, we need a new Jesus. But Jesus can handle that. He can handle everything you feel, and all your mistakes and flaws."

The same is true in your family.

Jesus can handle our smallest accidental mistakes as well as our greatest intentional sins.

If Jesus can't handle your kid's partying, we need a new Jesus.

If Jesus can't handle your kid's rebellion, we need a new Jesus.

But Jesus can handle it. He is our Savior because he can handle our sins and struggles, and so much more.

He can also handle your mistakes as a parent.

Parenting is by far my toughest role. My full-time job as the executive director of the Fuller Youth Institute is fairly demanding, but it's a piece of chocolate cake compared with being a parent.

As you read these pages, you're likely tired. You might even feel defeated. Although this is not at all my intention, reading the findings and ideas to help you be a Sticky Faith parent might unfortunately stoke your "I feel like a failure" fire.

Mom, Dad, Stepmom, Stepdad, Grandma, or Grandpa, please know this: Jesus is bigger than your mistakes too. On those days when you've failed to be the parent or grandparent you want to be, may this truth about Jesus help you learn from the past but not be imprisoned by it.

Sticky Findings

1 *Many Christian Young People Have Toxic Views of the Faith*

Unfortunately, too many young people—like those climbing on the branches of your family tree—have inaccurate and inadequate views of Jesus. Toward the end of our longitudinal study, we asked youth group graduates in their third year of college what it means to be a Christian. We were stunned by their answers.

Of the students who defined what it meant to be a Christian, one-third didn't mention Jesus.

You read that right. One-third didn't name Jesus.

What was the dominant answer? That being a Christian means we are supposed to "love other people."

Does Jesus want us to love other people? Of course he does.

But I could walk into the donut shop down the street and ask customers as they pour into the store, "Is it a good idea to love other people?" They would answer, "Yes." Surely there has to be something more robust beating at the heart of our faith. If our faith is only behaviors—even good behaviors like loving others—then no wonder young people aren't sticking with it. I wouldn't want to either.

As parents who want to expand and correct our kids' views of Christianity, we need to start by asking a central question: What distinguishes Christianity from all other religions? The immediate and obvious answer (and one that every third-grade Sunday school child knows is normally the right one) is "Jesus."

But let's peel back the layers and explore a bit more what makes Jesus different from Buddha, Joseph Smith, or Muhammad.

The answer is one word: grace.

Amazing grace.

Grace is what makes Christianity unique. In all other religions, you earn your salvation. There's a ladder of good works you climb to reach God's favor.

The life, death, and resurrection of Jesus smashes the ladder. Through the incarnation, God comes near to us, offering a gift of salvation that, like all true gifts, isn't dependent upon our actions, our goodness, or our ability to clean ourselves up. It's a gift we simply receive. And continue to receive as we stumble forward toward the author and perfecter of our faith.

2   Young People Run from God Just When They Need God the Most

Tragically, too many Christian young people still feel they have to climb the ladder of good behaviors in order to have a relationship with Jesus. They've embraced what Dallas Willard calls the "gospel of sin management"[1] — a reduction of the gospel to a checklist of do's and don'ts that allegedly helps them feel better about themselves and their relationship with God. As a result, kids end up more interested in doing and saying the right things (often with adults applauding their "Christian behaviors") than in seeking a genuine faith.

But invariably, no one can check off all the behavioral boxes. Your child will sin and struggle and fail to live up to their picture of what it means to be a "good Christian." It's not a matter of *if* but *when*.

During our research, I had a chance to speak with Rebecca, a student in our church's youth group when I was a junior high leader. The July before her eighth-grade year, Rebecca was one of the girls in my cabin at summer camp. Rebecca and I grew close that summer, but as she graduated a year later from middle school and then four years later from high school, we saw each other less and less.

Now a college graduate, Rebecca contacted me to find out more about Fuller Seminary. As both an alumna and a current faculty member at Fuller, I was thrilled not only that she was interested in studying with us but also that she wanted to have coffee and catch up.

For the first twenty minutes of our lively conversation, I answered her questions about Fuller's world-class programs and ministries. After I felt we had covered most of her interests, I broached a more personal topic. "Rebecca, I lost touch with you after you graduated from high school. We're studying what happens to youth group graduates as they head to college, and I'm wondering what that was like for you."

Rebecca had been giving me eye contact, but she immediately looked down at her coffee cup.

"Kara, it was really, really hard."

"Why?"

"Well, I started dating a non-Christian my freshman year of college," Rebecca said. "It was my experiment with 'missionary dating.' I went farther sexually than I ever thought I would. I felt so bad about what I had done that I plunged into an eating disorder and a depression."

Sitting across the table from Rebecca, I felt my heart breaking. But what she said next was even harder to hear.

"In the midst of how guilty I felt about how I had sinned, the last place I felt I could go for hope was the church. The last place I felt like I could turn to for healing was God."

Like many students we have interviewed these last ten years, somehow Rebecca had graduated from our church thinking that her

> I wish I had talked with my kids more about my failures, setbacks, and weaknesses. I didn't want my kids to know about my temptations. Looking back, I see that was a mistake.
>
> —Dwayne

faith was like a jacket—what we now call a "Jesus jacket." It's a jacket of behaviors that hasn't really changed young people from the inside out. When kids like Rebecca make poor choices, they feel they have tossed their Jesus jacket in the corner. What they don't understand is how to pick up that jacket, and even more important, that their faith is so much more than a coat of behaviors. Like Rebecca, instead of repenting and running back to God, they run away from a faith and a church that demand they worship a behavior-modification god.

3 Our Lives Are Great Big Thank-You Notes to God

But what about all the do's and don'ts in Scripture? If the gospel boils down to grace, what's the role of obedience in our kids' lives (as well as our own)?

Because of our studies revealing young people's false views of the gospel, my favorite way to explain the real gospel of Jesus Christ is through five words that start with the letter G. While you may have a different way of describing the gospel, part of why I

The Five Gs of the Gospel

Good	God created us good, in God's image.
Guilt	We then chose to disobey God, leaving us with the guilt of sin. All of us carry this mark, and it impacts us daily.
Grace	Through the life, death, and resurrection of Jesus, God has extended grace to us to make things right and restore us to relationship with God and one another.
God's people	As we experience grace, we are adopted into the body of Christ, embodying God's reign in the world. We join the mission of God, participating in the work of God happening through God's people.
Gratitude	Empowered by this gift of grace, we respond in gratitude toward God. Grace is the well out of which our obedience—those behaviors—flows. In other words, the Sticky gospel doesn't begin with behaviors, nor is it dependent on behaviors. The behaviors are like a big thank-you note we offer back to God in response to grace.

have adopted this version is that it's simple and memorable. Nine-year-olds can grasp it.

The first G word is *good*. All of us are created good, in God's image.

The second G is *guilt*. Our sin has separated us from God.

God couldn't stand that separation, so by God's *grace* (for those of you keeping score, that's the third G word), God sent Jesus to be crucified and resurrected so that we can repent of our sin and experience real life in the present as well as eternal life with him.

While this grace is central to our faith, it is not final. The fourth G is *God's people*. As we experience adoption into the body of Christ, we embody God's reign in the world. We join the mission of God, participating in the work of God happening through God's people.

The final G word, *gratitude*, helps connect the dots between the previous four Gs and the divine directives of Scripture. Why do we try to obey God's commands? It's not to make God love or like us more. It's not to feel better about ourselves.

It's because we're so full of gratitude. As I tell our three kids, our lives become great big thank-you notes to God for all that God has done for us.

Some days, you and I might not feel very grateful. We and our kids both have those seasons when we don't want to live as thank-you notes to God. In those moments, we circle back to the third G of grace. You and I need God's grace every day to live as he wants. We are fools if we think that in our own strength we can be the people or parents God wants us to be.

This obedient and grateful response is what separates true grace from what twentieth-century theologian Dietrich Bonhoeffer called "cheap grace." Cheap grace is a so-called grace that focuses on the beauty of God's goodness without shifting into conformity to God's will for our actions and attitudes. As Bonhoeffer summarizes, "Cheap grace is the preaching of forgiveness without requiring repentance, baptism without church discipline, Communion without confession.... Cheap grace is grace without discipleship, grace without the cross, grace without Jesus Christ, living and incarnate."[2]

Cheap grace is not grace at all.

I didn't make up these five Gs. They are based on a theological framework that emerged from the Heidelberg Catechism in the sixteenth century.

But even more important, they are rooted in the apostle Paul's own descriptions of the gospel. The early chapters of Paul's letters revolve around God's love, our sin, God's grace, and the power of community. The final chapters are typically where the bulk of the commands—the do's and don'ts—appear.

For instance, we see the progression of these five Gs in Paul's letter to the Ephesians. In Ephesians 1:4–5, Paul writes about how God has chosen, loved, predestined, and adopted us. (For those of you keeping score, that's the first G, *good*.) Yet in Ephesians 2:1–3, Paul warns that we were "dead in [our] transgressions and sins ... gratifying the cravings of our flesh," making us "deserving of wrath" (aka the second G, *guilt*). Yet because of God's mercy and love, when we repent and believe in Jesus, we are saved by God's grace (the third G) and made "alive with Christ" (Eph. 2:4–5). So now, as God's people (G number four), we are "fellow citizens with God's people and also members of his household" (Eph. 2:19), and we can experience "unity of the Spirit" (Eph. 4:3). And now, as "children of light" (Eph. 5:8), we are empowered to embrace the commands of the last chapters of Ephesians related to marriage, family relationships, and the armor of God (paralleling the fifth and final G, *gratitude*).

> *If faith is behaviors, then we expect our kids to be perfect and hide our own mistakes, claiming to be perfect. If faith is a journey, then mistakes are part of the process.*
>
> —Zeke

Being Sticky Faith parents means seeing all five of these Gs in our children. If we are unaware of the goodness of God's image in our children, we will never be able to love them as they need to be loved.

When we are blind to our kids' guilt, we lack the discipline and boundaries to tackle the dark and sinful sides of who they are and what they do.

We will never offer our kids the second, third, and seventeenth chances they need if we don't understand that God's grace does the same.

Without God's people, we wouldn't have the strength, encouragement, inspiration, and modeling we need to pursue relationship with Jesus and each other.

It is our sense of gratitude that points our kids to the potential they have to be changed by Christ to change the world around them.

4 The Contagious Power of "I'm Sorry"

In our fifty interviews, it became obvious that Sticky Faith parents are quick to apologize to their kids for their own mistakes. As one dad we interviewed confessed, "I've apologized to my daughters three times this week alone."

The transformational power of these apologies is captured by a family that is part of one of the congregations that nominated parents for our study. One Wednesday while the mom was in her teenage daughter's room, she found a used condom in her daughter's bed.

While this was challenging enough for the parents to navigate, it was even more complicated because two weeks prior both parents had told their daughter, "Your room is your room. It's your private space, and we will not enter it."

This mom and dad had basically told their daughter, "What happens in your room stays in your room." It was only because they violated that promise that they discovered the condom.

After praying and talking with their daughter's youth pastor, the parents decided that their first step was to repent before their daughter. The father approached his daughter later that night and confessed, "We made a mistake. We told you your room was your room, and we shouldn't

> It's easy to put on a good face for other people, but my kids live with me. It's hard to be a parent with authority and admit that I've messed up. I wish I had admitted that more, though.
>
> —Melody

have. We went into your room, and we shouldn't have. But we found something that we need to talk about."

Then they held their breath. They knew that they needed to have a heart-to-heart and very direct conversation about their daughter's dangerous choices but first they wondered how their daughter would feel about the fact that they had broken their promise to her. Would their daughter lash out because she felt betrayed and lied to? Or would their apology pave the way for candid and repentant conversation? Would their daughter lash out because she felt betrayed and lied to? Or would their apology pave the way for candid and repentant conversation?

They immediately got their answer. Their fifteen-year-old leaped into her dad's arms and confessed, "I'm so sorry, Dad."

After a few minutes of hugging her dad, she asked, "So what now?"

The dad answered, "Let's go get ice cream."

Over chocolate sundaes, they talked honestly. Mom and dad shared their deep concern over their daughter's sexual choices, their daughter further expressed her repentant desire to live a life of purity, and together they agreed on a plan that would hold her accountable for that purity.

I'm not implying that every time your children sin or struggle, you take them out for dessert. What I am saying is that if your families are like those of the parents we interviewed, when the going gets tough, you're more likely to have children who repent if you have made "I'm sorry" a regular part of your vocabulary.

5 ## Showing Grace Doesn't Mean Eliminating Boundaries

Right about now, you might be wondering if this Sticky Faith emphasis on grace means that we parents eliminate both behavioral boundaries for our kids as well as consequences for our kids when they cross those boundaries. After reading the previous story, you might be asking, Should kids sin all the more so that ice cream abounds?

Let me be clear: kids need boundaries. They need parents to

clearly lay out behavioral guidelines ahead of time and then discipline them when they step across those lines.

But wise Sticky Faith parents have found a way to sprinkle grace even into their discipline. Sometimes it's the tone of voice they use as they are taking away technology or certain other privileges.

Other times it's the way they empathize with their child's frustration—whether that is frustration the child feels over their

---

What if I'm struggling with forgiving my child?

If your child hasn't made you seeing-red mad, you haven't been a parent for long. Sometimes our kids burn so many bridges with us or others we care about that it's hard to know how to even start rebuilding the relationship. Sometimes our kids don't even seem sorry about the way they have tossed a grenade into our families, oblivious to the damage they have done to parents and siblings alike.

If you want to rebuild relationship with your child, perhaps an early step is to view your child not only as your offspring but also as a fellow follower of Jesus Christ and a part of your faith community, even if they may be currently unrepentant and in rebellion. In describing one of the keys to healthy community, Dietrich Bonhoeffer writes, "If my sinfulness appears to me to be in any way smaller or less detestable in comparison with the sins of others, I am still not recognizing my sinfulness at all.... My sin is the worst. He who would serve his brother in the fellowship must sink all the way down to these depths of humility."*

Bonhoeffer's description of his own sin parallels Paul's words in 1 Timothy 1:15: "Christ Jesus came into the world to save sinners—of whom I am the worst."

For both Paul and Bonhoeffer, the bad news of their sin made them more grateful for the good news of forgiveness through Jesus Christ. But the effects of their sin-awareness glasses didn't stop there. Their mindfulness of their depravity also changed the way they viewed others, making them quicker to embrace fellow sinners with love and compassion.

As you think about your family, ponder these three questions:

1. Are you aware enough of your selfishness to view yourself as the worst sinner in your household?

2. How would seeing more of your own sin expedite forgiveness in your family?

3. If your kid's mistakes have been so grave that you're feeling that these steps don't help at all, whom else could you seek for counsel to find a way forward?

*Dietrich Bonhoeffer, *Life Together* (New York: HarperCollins, 1954), 96.

own poor choice or (more likely) the frustration they feel with their mom or dad for imposing discipline.

Still other times, if they felt their child was truly repentant, a few parents we interviewed *every once in a while* erase the consequences of their kids' "crimes," explaining that "just as God shows us grace and mercy, I am going to show you grace and mercy."

While it's not easy to do, the remarkable parents we interviewed hold a ribbon of discipline in one hand and a ribbon of grace in the other, and somehow tie the two into a beautiful bow.

Sticky Ideas

The Note That Trumped the Lego Set

Pamela thought her son, Zachary, was strong-willed. Until Ethan was born. Parenting Ethan ushered Pamela into the big leagues of tantrums, power struggles, and the word *no* (a word she found herself saying and hearing more often).

One afternoon, seven-year-old Ethan's resistance to cleaning up his toys pushed one too many of Pamela's impatience buttons. She lashed out in anger. "Go to your room and stay there. I can't take you anymore." As Ethan slowly walked to his room, his hunched shoulders told Pamela that her words had caused him to question not just what he was doing but also how she felt about him.

While Pamela had always been quick to apologize to her boys, she knew Ethan needed a bolder gesture. She swung by the store and picked out a new Lego spaceship that Ethan had been eyeing. She paired the spaceship with a note that simply confessed, "Ethan, I am sorry for what I said. Will you forgive me? I love you. Mom."

To Pamela's surprise, Ethan barely played with the spaceship. Instead he clung to the note as the real treasure.

Now a college graduate, Ethan still has his mom's note. Despite moving in and out of multiple dorm rooms and even a few apartments, Ethan has kept his mom's tangible sign of repentance.

Your Family

- In what situations do you have the hardest time apologizing to your child?

- What past apology has meant the most to your child?

- The next time you blow it with your kid, how can you vividly and tangibly communicate that you are sorry and ask for their forgiveness?

The More Specific, the Better

Greg knows himself well enough to know that he tends to be pretty stubborn. While his tenacity has built profit in his company, it has eaten away at his relationship with his kids. The toughness that earns him promotions in the boardroom costs him at home.

Greg has learned that when he needs to apologize to his son or two daughters, he has to be specific. A vague "I'm sorry" accomplishes little. But his kids come to life when he gives more details, such as, "God has convicted me that I didn't honor you or respect you. If I want you to honor and respect me, I have to honor and respect you. Will you forgive me?"

> *What drives me crazy about my kids is what drives me crazy about myself. My daughter struggles with having a bad attitude. Guess who else also struggles with a bad attitude? Me. She has my DNA, so she has the best and worst of me.*
>
> —Eleanor

Your Family

- When you apologize to your kids, what do you usually say?

- How might being more specific, and perhaps even mentioning that God has convicted you about your sin, make a difference in your relationships with your kids?

No Statute of Limitations on Forgiveness

While we parents blow it on an almost daily basis, the reality is that we've been sinning every day since we were born. Sometimes the mistakes of previous years reach into today's calendar, affecting not only us but our kids too.

Gary never imagined he would get a divorce. While the decision to disband the marriage was his wife's, he still feels guilty for his role in his marriage's deterioration. Now his two young teenage children pay the price as they ping-pong back and forth every week between his house and his former wife's.

Many times Gary has explained to his children that divorce was never something he wanted or expected. His kids didn't cause the separation, and he hates that divorce is a reality of their lives.

As Gary has confessed his regrets to his kids, his kids have shown him grace. They have forgiven him for his role in their family's splintering. He feels that the remorse he has shown in front of his kids is part of his healing—and theirs too.

Your Family

- How are your past sins and mistakes possibly affecting both you and your kids?

- What role, if any, do you think talking about these realities with your kids might play in your family's healing and faith journey?

 ## The Mistake of the Day

In an effort to make mistakes a topic that their kids feel comfortable talking about, one family asks each night at the dinner table, "What mistake did you make today?" They laugh together over the story about how father and son headed to the wrong hockey rink, or the account of how mom's calendar confusion caused her to arrive at an important meeting fifteen minutes late.

Plus, the family's youngest member loves keeping track of her siblings' and parents' mistakes throughout the day. Whether the mom overfills the soap container or the dad forgets to set the house's overnight alarm, six-year-old Madison loves warning, "Oh boy, that's going to be your mistake of the day."

But even more important than those rather harmless blunders, talking about the day's mistakes gives the family a chance to confess their sins to each other and erase any hostility that has smudged their relationships. Whether it is the mom's tone of voice at the grocery store or the son's mean mocking of his sister's singing, sharing mistakes often leads to sharing apologies.

> *My daughter is thirteen and she's hormonal. I'm forty-seven and I'm hormonal.*
>
> —Mayra

Your Family

- How often do you talk about mistakes in your family? (Apart from someone needing to be disciplined; that doesn't count.)
- What could you do to try to make mistakes a more normal part of your daily conversation?

Long-Term Relationship = Long-Term Influence

As youth leaders at their church, Chuck and Helen have seen conflict erode far too many families in their congregation. Angry words and slammed doors cut off not just communication but also relationship. So Chuck and Helen have adopted a couple of mantras in their parenting:

1. As long as we have relationship with our kids, we have the potential for influence.
2. It is our responsibility as parents to keep the relationship with our children, not theirs.

Given these two ground rules, Chuck and Helen are determined to maintain relationship with each of their children, even while they discipline them. Or as Chuck and Helen would say, *especially* when they discipline them.

When eighth-grade Blake's report card meant he was grounded from all activities, including the upcoming baseball tournament, he stormed out of the family room and sequestered himself in his bedroom. While Helen knew it was right for Blake to be grounded, she also knew she needed to help Blake save face and give him a gracious entree back into the family. So she brought him popcorn and invited him to join them for dinner. Blake's shame and pride could have kept him in his room, cut off from the rest of the family for the night (even if he really would have rather come back downstairs). But Helen's initiative opened the door for Blake to leave his room and rejoin the family.

When getting ready to punish tenth-grade Suzanne for violating curfew by setting an earlier curfew for the next three weeks, Chuck told her, "What I'm about to tell you about your new curfew will make you mad, and I'm okay with that. You can say anything you want to me, but you have to do it in a respectful way." Chuck's message to his daughter was simple: You need to honor our rules, but I want to have a relationship with you no matter how you feel or what you say.

While other parents are tempted to subtract communication and relationship from their discipline strategies, Chuck and Helen try to add opportunities for conversation and connection.

Your Family

- What do you think of Chuck and Helen's two premises?
- What can you do in the midst of your family discipline to maximize conversation and relationship?

 ### Keep Calm and Carry On

The key to navigating discipline in Christine's family was that she told her three daughters ahead of time how she would respond to them when they told her they had blown it. If any of her kids told her what had happened themselves, they would face firm consequences, but those consequences would be merciful. If Christine found out herself from another source, the girls were then taking a gamble that she wouldn't be as gracious. The girls knew that if they were proactive in coming to their mom with their mistakes, they would be rewarded with a calm and compassionate mom.

Wanting to keep their mom calm, all three were fairly quick to talk to her about their everyday mistakes as well as their more egregious offenses. Not only did early conversation mean a more harmonious family, but it also meant that Christine could help her girls choose different paths before the ruts of their poor decisions grew too deep.

Your Family

- How do you tend to respond when your kids share their mistakes and sins with you?
- How does your typical response affect the likelihood that your kids will confess their struggles to you both early and often?

Our Family's Steps toward Sticky Faith

Take a few moments on your own, or with your spouse, your friends, or your small group, to reflect on some potential next steps toward Sticky Faith.

Sticky Findings

On a scale of 1 to 5 (with 1 being "we stink at this" and 5 being "we rock at this"), rate your family on the research findings presented in this chapter.

1| My kids understand that our faith is grounded in grace, not works.

① ② ③ ④ ⑤

2| My kids understand that Jesus is bigger than any mistake.

① ② ③ ④ ⑤

3| I regularly apologize to my kids when I blow it.

① ② ③ ④ ⑤

4| I clearly communicate behavioral boundaries to my kids, and my kids experience appropriate consequences when they cross those boundaries.

① ② ③ ④ ⑤

Sticky Ideas

1| In what ways is your family already permeated with a sense of repentance, forgiveness, and grace?

2| Given your ranking of the findings in the previous section, as well as the ideas you've read in this chapter, what one or two changes might you want to make in your family?

3| What can you do in the next few weeks or month to move toward these changes?

Chapter 4

Warm Family Relationships
Building Blocks of Sticky Faith

Bug spray. *Check.*

Sleeping bag. *Check.*

Hiking boots. *Check.*

Money for afternoon snacks. "Nathan, please go get my purse."

Nathan had been counting the weeks leading up to his first weekend Boy Scout camp. As we worked through the troop's recommended packing list, I knew there was one item I needed to add to our preparation. It had failed to make the master list but was just as important as extra socks.

It was a heart-to-heart discussion about pornography.

A few years prior, I had asked my husband when he first had been exposed to pornography. He was twelve at a Boy Scout camp when a sixth-grade tentmate pulled out a magazine.

Our son was now twelve. And headed to a Boy Scout camp.

So after rounding up a flashlight and first-aid kit, Dave and I sat on the edge of Nathan's bed and talked with him about pornography— what it is and how he could respond. We brainstormed what he could do and say. (Sport-loving Nathan's favorite response was, "I'd rather go play basketball.") We even did some role-playing.

Yes, it's that fun growing up in the Powell family.

The morning of camp, I wanted to send Nathan off with some final words from me, words of encouragement and inspiration. I stopped him outside of his bedroom door, put my arm on his shoulder, and said, "Nathan, there are two things I want you to know."

Smiling, Nathan looked up at me and guessed, "I'm awesome."

I smiled back. "Okay, Nathan, there are *three* things I want you to know about camp. Number one: you're awesome. Number two: your dad and I think you're going to make good decisions. Number three: even when you struggle, God likes and loves you, and we like and love you too."

In the previous chapter, we looked at how Sticky Faith parents communicate to their children that God is fond of them, even when they blow it. In this chapter, we'll zoom in on how these same parents communicate a parallel message to their children as early as possible: "Not only is God fond of you; we're crazy about you too." The affection we demonstrate to our children can plant seeds that bear fruit for years to come, not only in their relationships with us but also in their relationships with God.

Sticky Findings

1 | *The Power of Warmth*

One study of relational dynamics in more than three hundred families, spanning thirty-five years, analyzed the power of warmth among the generations. Family warmth was more correlated with faith transmission than any other relational factor (including the amount of contact children had with their parents or grandparents, the type of contact, and the number of children in the family). Families in which parents and children felt close were more likely to be families in which children adopted the faith of their parents.[1] This was found to be true not just in evangelical and mainline Protestant families but in Jewish and Mormon families as well.

2 Special Daddy Bond

While both parents are important in creating a warm family atmosphere, fathers may be the more important relational barometer. For instance, in evangelical Protestant families, 46 percent of children who feel "not close" to their fathers report that they have adopted the same faith as their parents. For children in evangelical Protestant families who feel "close" to their fathers, that rate jumps to 71 percent. That 25 percent gap in faith adoption dwarfs the 1 percent gain in faith adoption between children who feel "close" to their mothers and those who feel "not close" to them.

> Wondering what might be unique about moms in building Sticky Faith? We'll dive into that in chapter 8.

This differential between maternal and paternal warmth also exists in mainline Protestant families, although not quite as dramatically. Children from mainline Protestant families who feel "close" to their fathers have a 17 percent gain in adopting the faith of their parents compared with those who feel "not close" to their fathers. Mainline Protestant children who feel "close" to their mothers have a 3 percent gain in following in the faith footsteps of their parents compared with those who feel "not close" to their mothers.[2]

3 It's How Close Your Child Feels to You That Counts

Regardless of your gender, do you think you know how close you are to your child? Maybe, but maybe not.

In the same longitudinal study of families over thirty-five years, parents typically ranked their relationships with their children as more intimate and cohesive than their children did.[3] Researchers found that a child's *perception* of closeness matters more than the parent's perception of closeness. Your child is likely to be a more stringent grader of your family relationships, and their grade counts more than yours.

What if I feel "unwarm" toward my child?
What about when my child just ticks me off?

Smiling. Singing. Playing creative games with our children.

No parent can adhere to the cheerful picture of parenting painted by Julie Andrews in *The Sound of Music*. Instead of making playclothes out of curtains and producing lively puppet shows, we are bound to get frustrated and downright angry over our kids' attitudes and actions. How do we handle those feelings in ways that are healthy for ourselves and our families? Perhaps one or more of these suggestions will help:

Determine whether you are getting the rest you need. Personal confession from me: I am twice as good of a parent when I am more rested and less stressed. At least half of the frustration I feel toward and show my kids happens on those days when I don't have enough emotional or logistical margin.

Examine whether your own issues are contributing to your frustration. Often we parents overreact to our kids when we see qualities in them that we don't like in ourselves. Perhaps your frustrations with your moody son or overly dramatic daughter are more about what you wish you could change in yourself than what you wish you could change in them.

Remember that what bothers you about your child is likely also something you love about them. You love your son's independence but wish he'd be friendlier to other kids his age. You treasure your daughter's quick wit but wish she weren't so sarcastic. God has given your child amazing strengths they are figuring out how to use; in the process, your child often goes overboard. Talk with your child about what you love about them and walk alongside them as they figure out how to be who God has made them to be—no more and no less.

As your children move into adolescence, view them with compassion. It's normal and healthy for teenage children to go through an extended season of "individuation," meaning they are becoming individuals with an independent identity that builds upon but is separate from their family identity. You may have more compassion when you realize it's developmentally normal for them to push and pull on the emotional and relational strings that connect you to them.

Analyze your discipline strategy. If you're finding that your discipline system isn't working with your family, maybe you need a new strategy. Your consequences may have fit one age level but are too lenient or strict for your child's new developmental stage.

Listen to your spouse or close friends. None of us has 20/20 vision when it comes to our own parenting. Ask your spouse or close friends what they think might turn up the warmth in your family relationships.

Have a heart-to-heart with your kids. Many of the Sticky Faith parents we interviewed weren't afraid to bring up tough subjects with their kids. In fact, they viewed those discussions as opportunities to strengthen both family communication and family relationships. If your family is experiencing more strife than normal, take your kids out for dessert and talk about why that might be happening. Without blaming any single family member, brainstorm the type of family relationships you'd like to have and what you all could do differently to make that vision a reality.

Do something fun together. Some weeks, the time we spend with our kids consists only of busy mornings trying to get everyone out of the house, and tired evenings when we're all blasted from the day. Perhaps what your family needs in order to regain a more harmonious rhythm is a few hours of fun together.

Know when you need outside help. If your norm is constant conflict with one or more of your children, it might be time to get outside help from a professionally trained therapist, counselor, or pastor. Regardless of whether it's appropriate for that advisor to meet with your child, start with yourself. Your discussions with the right person can unearth the roots of what's bothering you and lead to greater peace for you—and maybe your family too.

Sticky Ideas

 ## Family Meetings

After dinner on Tuesdays, the Wellborn family clears the dishes from the table and then sits back down for their weekly family meeting. Tom and Marcia started these meetings to give their family a chance to share their perspectives on what's going well—and not so well—in their household. It has also become a time to review the week ahead so everyone understands the logistics of science projects and softball car pools.

Often the meeting has a theme question, like, How can we be more of a team? or, Why have we not been nice to each other this week? But sometimes the discussion bounces from topic to topic— from dinner leftovers to a child who's feeling left out.

Some family meetings are long; others last only a few minutes.

Sometimes one of the children brings a current event for the family to pray about together; other times the meetings end with family members sharing personal prayer requests and praying aloud for each other.

> I wish we had done a better job helping our kids look for answers to their prayers. We lift all sorts of things to God in prayer, but are we coming back around and recognizing God's answers?
>
> —Jeremy

Occasionally the four Wellborns study Scripture or memorize a Bible verse together. But truth be told, most of the time they don't.

Usually the kids seem to enjoy the family meetings, but when their enthusiasm wanes, Tom and Marcia ask their kids how they could improve their time together.

In the midst of the variety offered, Tom and Marcia strive to make one quality universal in all of their family meetings: "We make sure the kids know they have a voice and can share their experiences, so they know their feelings matter."

Your Family

- What, if any, sort of regularly scheduled communication do you have with your children?

- How do you think some sort of regular meeting would benefit your family?

- If even the term "family meeting" feels overly structured to you, what sorts of gatherings would best fit your family and give your children a voice in your family decisions?

 ## Don't Fight or Mom Will Make Us Hold Hands

While clashes between parents and children can cause families' "warmth temperature" to fall a few degrees, equally problematic can be conflict among kids. Many families find that fights among siblings are more frequent—and more chilling—than any other form of family conflict.

One creative mom we interviewed came up with a way to

prevent her young kids from fighting: when they get into disagreements, she makes them hold hands. She gives them full opportunity to air their grievances and frustrations with each other, but they have to do it while holding hands.

During a long car trip, this mom overheard the initial backseat rumblings of a potential fight between her two sons. But the eight-year-old quickly told his six-year-old brother, "Don't fight. Mom will make us hold hands."

Your Family

- How does your typical response to your kids' sibling skirmishes help—or hinder—your ability to relate tenderly to them?
- This family found that holding hands got their kids' attention and made them less likely to fight with each other. What dramatic step could you take that would accomplish the same in your family?

 ## Annual Overnighters

As a youth leader, I often tell families that a student who attends a weekend retreat experiences the relational equivalent of attending Sunday school for six months. In more than twenty-five years of student ministry, I've found nothing that bonds adults and kids more than time away.

The Sticky Faith parents we interviewed often capitalize on that same "overnight mojo" to build stronger bonds with their kids.

These overnighters aren't all that expensive or glamorous. Parents use the time to play games, make forts in hotel rooms, explore local neighborhoods, or dive deeper into family discussions over ice cream or pancakes. But when you're eight years old, any room with a TV and an ice machine down the hall is a thrill, even if it's a two-star hotel fifteen minutes from your house that your dad found online. But what the overnighters sometimes lack in charm and room decor, they more than make up for in conversation and memories.

Your Family

- What has happened in your family when you've been able to do overnighters away from home or in your back yard or even "camping" in your living room?
- Is it realistic for you to budget the time and money required to do a special overnighter with all your children, or perhaps one child at a time, sometime in the next year?

 ## Special Seasons

Sticky Faith parents seem to look for reasons — maybe even excuses — for celebrations and date nights with their kids. Blanca initiated a "seasonal date" tradition with her son, Emilio. Four times a year — at the start of winter, spring, summer, and fall — Blanca takes Emilio out for an after-school or dinner date.

Sometimes Blanca and Emilio engage in an activity that's related to the start of the season. They'll search for the prettiest autumn leaf they can find in September or the best bouquet of wildflowers they can pick in March.

Other times they get sushi and share highlights of the past three months and dreams for the next three months. Regardless of what they do, this quarterly time together gives both Blanca and Emilio a sense that not only is the year unfolding, but so is their relationship.

Your Family

- For those of you who live in regions where the weather is dramatically different from season to season, what family ritual might you want to start?
- For those of you who live in regions without much weather variation, are there other annual rhythms (perhaps connected with your kids' school calendars) that would be more vivid?

Same Prayer, Every Day

Before their oldest was even born, Adam and Robyn asked God how they should be praying for their kids. After thinking about their own individual strengths and combined passions, Adam and Robyn felt led to pray that their children would be people who

> know God loves them,
> love and serve God and others,
> lead and learn,
> are gentle but strong,
> are content but take risks.

Starting while their children were in utero, Adam and Robyn have prayed this prayer every day for their kids, now ages ten, eight, and five. The kids have it memorized and sometimes pray it aloud with them. While it can feel a bit rote at times, Adam and Robyn love that their kids know they asked God to show them how to pray even before their kids were born.

Your Family

- What prayers tend to be most meaningful to your children?
- If you have a prayer (even a sentence or two) that you privately pray for your children, how might sharing that prayer with them show them how much you care?

Baptism Birthday

Alfredo and Susanna's denomination encourages infant baptism as an early sign that the children are joining the covenant community. To help their three children remember and celebrate their baptism, Alfredo and Susanna throw each child an annual baptism birthday party.

Alfredo and Susanna invite the same godparents who were present at the baptism to dinner on that child's baptism anniversary. They request that the godparents bring a Scripture text with them

My wife is great at throwing family celebrations. For birthdays, she makes big posters and hangs up banners around our house. We've also experienced illness in our family; our oldest son has had cancer three times. Once when he finished his chemotherapy regimen, my wife threw a big party for him with our family and friends in the hospital room. In that time of real sadness, it was also a time of real joy that he had finished that treatment and we were able to celebrate with him.

—Bruce

that summarizes their hopes and prayers for that child for the next year.

On the night of the baptism birthday, the family enjoys a dinner menu selected by the child being honored (which tends to mean a lot of hot dogs, pizza, and macaroni and cheese). Alfredo and Susanna retell the child's baptism story, and the godparents present the verse for the year. The end of the meal is marked with cake and prayer.

No gifts are given, but it ends up being as exciting to the child as their actual birthday. Next to each child's bed is a framed photo of their baptism in which the Scripture text for the new year is inserted. While the three children don't remember the day of their baptism, they are surrounded by reminders of the people who loved them that day and continue to love them today.

Your Family

- For those of you whose faith tradition includes infant baptism, what might you do annually to commemorate that baptism?
- For those of you who don't practice infant baptism, what other rituals (such as baby dedication, First Communion, or baptism later in life) could be celebrated and honored every year?

Birthday Dates

While Gabe valued his time with all three of his kids together, he found a special connection when he had only one pair of eyes looking at him instead of three. He liked the idea of one-on-one monthly time with each kid, but he needed a scheduling tool to make sure it didn't slip through the calendar cracks.

So Gabe started doing monthly birthday dates. His second-grader was born on May 8, so on the eighth of every month, his second-grader gets an hour with just dad. An hour alone to do whatever he wants, whether that is play a board game, go on a hike, or grab an ice cream cone. The same is true for his fourth-grader on the fourteenth and his fifth-grader on the twenty-seventh.

It is three hours out of Gabe's month that Gabe has never missed. Even if he wanted to, his children wouldn't let him.

Your Family

- Given that you have limited time with your children, what balance would you like to strike between time with all of your kids together and one-on-one time?

- What made Gabe so effective is that he went from a vague "I'd like to get together with each kid monthly" to a specific plan and a specific date. If the birthday date doesn't work for your family, how can you move from good intentions to actually scheduling time with your kids?

 ## Monthly Conversation Journals

Gabe was not the only parent we interviewed who desired a monthly date with each of his children. Inspired by what they had heard about Sticky Faith, the Bonner family decided not only to schedule regular one-on-one times with their kids but also to keep a timeless record of those conversations and experiences together.

So Donny and Andrea let both of their kids select a journal from a local office supply store. Their monthly one-on-one dates always involved something fun (like playing tennis, baking brownies for a neighbor, or heading to a movie) as well as a good conversation. Over smoothies or lunch, each parent would ask whichever child was with them questions like, What's your favorite thing about our family? What would you change about our house? Which friend would you like to get to know better? The parent would jot down not only the questions but also their kid's answers.

Then it was the child's turn to ask questions. Most of their questions were pretty tame, such as, What do you do at your job? or, What's your favorite restaurant?

But at times the child's questions gave Andrea or Donny a poignant (and often painful) glimpse into the kid's psyche that they wouldn't otherwise have. Like the time when their daughter asked Donny, "Why are you working so much at night?" Or when their son asked Andrea, "Why don't we sit down together at dinner anymore?"

Those questions and answers were also noted in the journals. When not in use on their family dates, those two journals stood proudly on the Bonners' living room bookshelf, a constant reminder of the family members' rich time together.

> *While I love planned outings with my kids, I've found that some of my best conversations happen impromptu — when my kids are ready to have them. The question I have to ask myself is, Am I willing to interrupt my schedule because my kid just said something completely bizarre or powerful?*
> —Kenneth

Your Family

- For some parents, writing down notes from a conversation feels too formal and stuffy. If that's the case for you, how can you commemorate and remember those special times and discussions with your children?

- What questions do you think your kids might want to ask you? Instead of guessing, how about grabbing some hot chocolate and asking them to share questions they have for you or your family?

 ## Celebrating Your Family Heritage

For Paul and Yuna, building a warm, intimate relationship with their children means celebrating their family heritage. Yuna is Korean-American; Paul is an Anglo-Saxon, Greek, Messianic Jew. When it comes to playing the race or ethnicity card, their three elementary-age children have quite a full hand.

While Paul and Yuna view their children first and foremost as followers of Jesus, they also want them to have a strong sense of their cultural roots. To fulfill that goal, every year Paul and Yuna invite fifteen or so friends over to observe the Messianic Passover. To help their children connect with their dad's Jewish history, Paul and Yuna involve their children in all aspects of the ceremony, from preparation ahead of time to specific roles during the ceremony and discussions afterward.

Paul and Yuna also introduce their kids to Greek and Korean language, food, and even dress, all to help their kids learn about and enjoy every facet of who they are and who their family is. For Paul and Yuna, exposing their kids to the vast and varied branches of their family tree is part of what bonds them to their family members both past and present.

Your Family

- If you have divergent cultural currents that unite in your family, how do you try to honor those various and beautiful streams that make you who you are?
- If your family is more monocultural, how can you help your children come to appreciate that particular culture?
- How might increased appreciation for your family's cultural background make a difference in your family relationships?

A Soccer Goal for an Ice Cream

Scott loved watching his stepsons play soccer. For many parents, AYSO (American Youth Soccer Organization) stands for "All Your Saturdays Occupied." For Scott, it represented a chance to show his stepsons that he cared about them and that he was proud of them.

Soccer came naturally for Scott's oldest, ten-year-old Trevor. It was the rare game in which Trevor didn't score a goal.

But for eight-year-old Devon, soccer was more of a struggle. It wasn't that he was bad; it was just that he wasn't particularly good. If there were a medal for mediocrity, it would have been Devon's.

In an effort to motivate his stepsons to try their hardest, Scott told them that each soccer goal they scored would be worth ice cream for the family. Both boys loved this idea, largely because they knew that Trevor could score lots of goals.

Devon went scoreless for the first few games, but that was okay. Trevor was scoring enough to make up for it. Not a weekend went by without ice cream. As Scott and his two sons celebrated over these treats, Scott found it easy to verbally recount Trevor's soccer prowess.

This ice cream ritual seemed to be working. Or so Scott thought, until one day on the way home from yet another score-less game for Devon, when Devon said somewhat quietly in the back seat, "Scott, I know I don't do that well in sports, but do you realize that you have never, not once, told me that I've done well?"

Scott's heart plummeted. He had been so well intentioned, but the ice cream ritual had backfired. Scott's effort to affirm his step-sons' accomplishments had done the opposite. He had intended the treat to be a tangible reminder of his love for them, but instead it sent the message that his love and affirmation was something Devon needed to earn. Scott had unknowingly set a high bar, a bar that Devon thought he would never be able to clear. And Devon was probably right.

Scott immediately revised his ice cream policy. He now takes out both boys for ice cream every game day, regardless of whether either of them scored. As they sit on the curb, cones in hand, Scott compliments *both* boys on their accomplishments and their attitudes.

Your Family

- In the midst of rewards you've offered for sports or school, in what ways might you have unintentionally communicated that your love is conditional or that your approval is based on what your children do?

- What can you do to show your children that you are crazy about them whether they succeed or fail?

Warm and Fuzzy Bedtime

Many of the Sticky Faith parents we interviewed find bedtime a "yummy" (to quote one mom) time to connect with their elementary-age children. Some of the ideas our team found most noteworthy are:

- Singing the doxology together so that the children know that "singing to the Lord is a natural thing."
- Keeping a family journal that tracks what they've prayed about at night and how God has answered those prayers.
- Reading together from a children's Bible.
- Learning Scripture together. (One family started teaching their kids nighttime Bible verses at age two.)
- Asking their children, especially later in elementary school, "How's your heart?"

Perhaps the most vivid example of bedtime tenderness came from one dad who sings a couple of songs each night to his son, often rubbing his son's back while he sings. Those two songs (one of which his dad made up to boast about how much he loves his son) and that backrub are a tradition that has lasted every night for thirteen years. Now at age fourteen, the son still asks for those two songs and a backrub every night.

As the dad described, "That's the most intimate time each day we have with our son. If I end up somehow skipping it, our son will come into our room an hour after bedtime and say, 'I can't get to sleep. You haven't sung to me yet.'"

Okay, moment of confession: When I'm really tired at bedtime, I breeze through our normal rituals. One time instead of waiting until I had tucked my daughter into her cozy bed, I actually prayed with her while she was brushing her teeth.

—Amber

Your Family

- What nighttime rituals are most meaningful to your family? How are they already creating a sense of warmth and connection in your relationships with your kids?

- What other ideas do you have that might make your bedtime conversations even more special?

- After a long day at work or home, it may be hard to muster the energy to really connect with your kids at night. If that's true for you, what could you do in the few hours before your kids head to bed to save up your energy for these late-night rituals?

Our Family's Steps toward Sticky Faith

Take a few moments on your own, or with your spouse, your friends, or your small group, to reflect on some potential next steps toward Sticky Faith.

Sticky Findings

On a scale of 1 to 5 (with 1 being "we stink at this" and 5 being "we rock at this"), rate your family on the research findings presented in this chapter.

1| Our relationships with our kids are characterized by loving warmth.

① ② ③ ④ ⑤

2| While we recognize that warm relationships with both parents are important, our kids have a close relationship with their dad (or stepdad or another adult male).

① ② ③ ④ ⑤

3| Our kids would say that our family has close, supportive relationships.

① ② ③ ④ ⑤

Sticky Ideas

1| What do you already do to build close, loving relationships with your children?

2| Given your ranking of the findings in the previous section, as well as the ideas you've read in this chapter, what one or two changes might you want to make in your family?

3| What can you do in the next few weeks or month to move toward these changes?

Chapter 5

Connecting

Finding Ways to Relate to Your Teenager

"What if my teenager doesn't want to spend time with me?"

It's a common question, one our team is asked almost every time we share the secrets of Sticky Faith families.

My favorite answer is to share the story of Nora, a mom who has used our research to bridge the divide with her son. Seventeen-year-old Sam walled himself off from Nora and the rest of the family eighteen months ago. The only time Sam leaves his room is when he's hungry (which, luckily for Nora, is often). But when she tries to start up a conversation while Sam's standing in front of the refrigerator or the microwave, she's greeted with one-syllable answers: "Fine," "Nope," or "Uh-uh."

Longing for a deeper relationship, Nora has tried to connect with Sam. But every time she offers to take him out for a meal or do something fun, he refuses. He'd rather shut himself in his room and go online or play video games than be with her.

But Sam does love going to movies.

So Nora has become a student of film. She tracks movie release dates, visits movie websites, and has learned the nuances of various directors and actors.

The only time Sam says yes to Nora's invitations to do something with her is when she asks Sam to a movie. On the way to the movie, the two of them discuss what they know about the film and what they hope it will be like. Driving home, they evaluate the movie and share their favorite scenes. At times Sam even opens up about connections he sees between the film and his own experiences. The roundtrip conversation is Nora's best window into her son's life and heart.

Because of this, Nora tries to pick theaters that are far away, so they have more time in the car together.

She also tries to suggest movies that have a spiritual flavor. Hints of spiritual growth in the films' characters occasionally prompt Sam to talk about his spiritual journey—at least for a few sentences.

Nora doesn't really like movies all that much, but she likes her son. As with the majority of the Sticky Faith parents we interviewed, Nora is willing to leave the well-worn path of her own comfort and preferences to journey with her teenager.

Sticky Findings

1 ## It's More about Your Teenager's World Than Yours

One of the most dominant themes in our interviews with parents was their commitment to step into their teenagers' worlds instead of expecting their kids to take part in theirs.[1] They take seriously Paul's words in 1 Thessalonians 2:8: "Because we loved you so much, we were delighted to share with you not only the gospel of God but our lives as well." They know that the sharing Paul describes often means leaning into their kids' interests and passions. For Nora, that means becoming a movie aficionado.

For Chris, that translates into making a TV reality show (one of the few he can stomach) a popcorn-and-hot-chocolate family event every Thursday night.

For Hany, that means letting his son play his favorite music in the car. Hany can barely stand his son's song selections, but he sees his son stand a bit taller when he knows that his dad cares about what he cares about.

Multiple studies conducted by the Search Institute and other academic partners indicate how motivating it is for young people to discover their "sparks," meaning the activities and interests that help kids be their best. Two of the most common sparks for young people are sports and art, and yet only 55 percent of teenagers who know their sparks receive adult support for the development and use of those passions and skills.[2]

The parents we interviewed were trying to buck this trend by verbally encouraging their kids' interests, being physically present, and even participating when possible. Even if parents are ignored by their daughter at the school play or are sought out by their son at the lacrosse tournament only when he wants cash for snacks, they

> *Whatever our kids did, we showed up. We volunteered in Scouts, bands, and sports. We kept showing up. We kept being involved.*
> —Bennett

are in the stands, cheering for their kids. Those choices to make it to three o'clock games or seven o'clock shows often come at a professional cost. Whenever possible, Sticky Faith parents pay that price because they are committed to making regular deposits in their teenagers' emotional bank accounts.

2 *Family Time Together Needs to Be Protected*

A second theme in our interviews with fifty Sticky Faith parents was that they set firm walls around their time with their teenage children. In fact, as a research team, we joked about how practically every parent of teenagers we interviewed noted that time together is key to their family's faith.

Middle schoolers are far more busy than elementary school children. That busyness escalates in high school. Parents who want to maintain relationship with their teenage children make sure that they carve out quality time together.

As our friends Reggie Joiner and Carey Nieuwhof wisely describe in *Parenting beyond Your Capacity*, "It's not quantity or quality time you need as a family—it's the *quantity of quality time*. ... When you increase the quantity of quality time you spend together as a family, you leverage your ability to positively impact your children's faith."[3]

To amass a large amount of quality time, Sticky Faith parents work hard to coordinate all family members' calendars to make sure they are all regularly in the same house, sitting in the same room, at the same time.

3. Sticky Faith Families Have Both Planned and Spontaneous Time Together

A ten-year-old is pretty much open to being with her dad anytime he says, "Let's play catch." Fast-forward five years, and that same dad's offer to play catch is generally met with a "Not now, Dad" response. (The primary exception being if the dad offers to go shopping instead of stand in the front lawn throwing a ball back and forth.)

Relationship now happens on the teenager's terms. So in addition to the more structured times encouraged in the previous finding, the Sticky Faith parents we interviewed also keep their schedules free enough that they can dive into more informal, organic time together. Dads find they need to sit at the kitchen table while their son has a "second dinner" after basketball practice, waiting to see if he'll open up about his day. Moms stop using a cell phone in the car if their daughter is along, in case she wants to talk about the anxiety she's feeling about her upcoming finals.

These unstructured times happen only if parents have created enough margin in their schedules to be nearby when their teenage children want to talk. As defined by Richard A. Swenson, "Margin is the amount allowed beyond that which is needed. . . . Margin is the gap between rest and exhaustion, the space between breathing freely and suffocating."[4] The families we studied reported regularly having to make decisions—hard decisions—that cost them professionally, economically, and socially in order to have the time and energy required to be present with their teenagers when their teenagers want to talk.

4 *Favoritism May Erode Faith*

If you're a parent of multiple children, you may be wondering, Why is it that kids in the same family sometimes walk down diverging faith paths? If we parent our teenagers similarly, why would they make different choices?

Many factors can contribute to differences among siblings, ranging from unique personalities and particular stressful experiences to birth order and openness to the Spirit. Yet one body of research suggests that while we think we treat our children fairly and similarly, our children don't feel that way.

A recent study of 156 members of twenty-five different families found that the most common theme in children who walked away from their parents' faith was that they thought their parents played favorites. As a result, not only did rivalry develop among the siblings, but also teenagers who felt mistreated tried to separate themselves from all things related to their parents, including their parents' faith.[5]

Sticky Ideas

 Family Game Nights

Of the variety of ways Sticky Faith parents spent time with their teenagers, one of the most common is family game nights. Parents who want to fuel the flames of family game nights tend to

- keep games in a central place in their homes.
- continually add new board games to their family collection.
- look for games that all family members can play together (which isn't always easy, given age gaps among kids).
- serve special snacks.
- integrate outdoor games when possible (weather allowing).

One mom, whose youngest of four children is now entering college, told us, "We just did a game night with all of our kids home for the holidays this past weekend. Our boys hate games without strategy. Our girls hate games that are too competitive. So we've worked hard to find games that work for all four. Some of our best family memories come from sitting on the floor playing games together."

Your Family

- What place do games have in your family's quality time?
- If you're not satisfied with your answer, what would help games play more of a central role in your family time together?

 ## Talking about Your Future Spouse

Marianne wanted to connect with Kylie, her stepdaughter, on Kylie's terms but wasn't sure how to do it. She got her answer when Kylie started asking Marianne questions about why she had decided to marry Kylie's dad.

Kylie's questions told Marianne that she was starting to wonder not just about Marianne's relationship with Kylie's dad but also about what her own future husband might be like. Marianne gave Kylie a journal and encouraged her, "When you see a characteristic that you want in your husband, write that down in this journal." Periodically Marianne and Kylie bring the journal along to coffee and discuss what Kylie has noted. This journaling has both helped Kylie process her residual pain from her parents' divorce and helped plant in her a clearer and more hopeful vision for her future family.

Your Family

- Marianne wisely let Kylie's questions reveal what was important to Kylie. Thinking back on the past few months, what themes have you noticed in your teenagers' conversations or questions?
- How can you leverage those themes as ways to spend time with your kids?

Getting Ready to Be an Adult

If there's one thing (almost) every adolescent wants, it's to be treated as an adult. Capitalizing on the way his oldest son, Quan, almost salivated at the idea of being treated like a grown-up, Jun told him that before he could be treated like an adult, he had to act like one.

So Jun and Quan started a series of "adult projects" together. Jun taught Quan everything from car maintenance to composting. The teenager learned how to shop for groceries, cook a few basic meals that reflect his Chinese culture, and thoroughly clean the kitchen. He was tutored by his dad in how to fill the dishwasher and the clothes dryer. Jun increased Quan's allowance but also made Quan responsible for more of his own expenses. Quan was required both to give away 10 percent of what he received and to calculate how to divide the remaining 90 percent among clothes, food, and entertainment. Jun met regularly with his son so they could evaluate together how he was doing with his adult responsibilities. Quan's younger siblings watched this process closely, eager for a foretaste of what awaited them.

Normally Quan would have balked at the idea of spending so much time with his dad, but learning to be an adult was a powerful motivation. Quan still grumbled about some of the chores, but not nearly as much as normal. Jun was doubly blessed—not only did he get exponentially more time with his son, but also he knew he was preparing Quan for what he would face after he left home.

Your Family

- What might motivate your teenager to learn new skills and take on new responsibilities?
- How could your time mentoring them in these new tasks build your relationship?

Mom Reads Harry Potter First

Maggie was thrilled that her four kids all loved to read. But she was less thrilled at the prospect of her kids diving into books that might not be developmentally appropriate for them.

So Maggie created a new policy: before her kids read a book, she has to read it (or at least skim it). Maggie recalls, "There have been many years when I didn't read a single book that I chose. I'm a reader myself, so it was a sacrifice to spend so much time in just my kids' books."

What makes the sacrifice worth it for Maggie? Not only does she get windows into teenage culture, but also she uses her teenagers' books as conversation starters. She often places sticky notes on pages she wants to talk over with her kids. Her kids know that when they come across one of those sticky notes, they have to stop reading and find Mom to talk with her about what is going to happen next in the story. By diving into her kids' love for literature (if you can call novels about middle school friendships "literature"), Maggie is able to better navigate the cultural rivers flowing through her teenagers' lives.

Your Family

- If any of your teenagers like to read, how would reading some of the same books add more depth to your relationship?

- For those of you whose teenagers aren't prone to reading, how would watching some of their favorite TV shows, playing their preferred video games, or listening to their top music help you better connect with them?

 ## How Can I Pray for You?

Tammi wants her teenage boys to know that not only is she willing to spend time with them talking about God, but she also spends time every day talking to God about them. So she asks her two sons a simple question: How can I be praying for you? She either writes down their answers or asks them to do so.

She keeps the sheets they have written in her prayer journal, but she makes copies to give back to her boys so they have reminders of her specific prayers for them. By asking this simple question, Tammi learns more about her boys' struggles and dreams, and her boys learn more about their mom's passion for prayer.

Your Family

- What's your best current way to share with your kids your prayers for them?
- How much do you share with your teenagers about what you're praying for them?
- What might asking your teenagers for prayer requests and then giving them a written copy of those requests communicate to them?

 ## An Eighth-Grade Prayer

Before storming down the hallway to his bedroom, Andrew yelled at Allison, "Mom, I'm tired of you, and I'm tired of this family. You just don't understand me."

While feeling misunderstood is common to teenagers, Allison took an uncommon response. She viewed Andrew's tantrum as an opportunity to learn more about the source of his anger. After a few minutes, she knocked on his bedroom door, walked in, and they had a long conversation about all Andrew was keeping from his mom. Like how school is a "pressure cooker," church is a place where he "has no friends," and at home his parents "focus more on his brother than on him." Neither Andrew nor Allison cried, but they both came close.

To wrap up their conversation, Allison prayed a simple prayer with Andrew: "Lord, let us love you more, let us love each other more, and please fill us with your Holy Spirit."

That one sentence became Allison and Andrew's special prayer. Through high school, they prayed it every day together, generally at night. Now Andrew is away at college, but when he comes home for vacation, they pray that same prayer together.

Allison has a different prayer with her other son, Charlie. She loves that her boys know they have a special spiritual connection both with their mom and with Christ.

Your Family

- What have you learned about your teenager when they showed you their anger, sadness, or fear?
- How would having a special prayer with each of your kids affect your relationships with them?

LOL = Loving Online

Entering into teenagers' worlds means using the technology they use. In chapter 10, we'll talk more about how Sticky Faith parents have set boundaries on their family's use of technology. But creative parents also see technology as one of the best ways to enter their kids' worlds. Innovative parents use technology such as texting and social media to

My mom saw clients at her job, so she couldn't always take my calls. But my dad would always answer the phone if he saw it was me, even in important business meetings.

—Mia

- let their kids know they are available for them at any time.
- tell their kids they're thinking of them.
- remind their kids that they are praying for them, given what they are facing at school that day.
- share a Bible verse, maybe inserting their child's name in the passage.
- chat with their kids onscreen while they are out of town.
- send pictures of what they are seeing or eating, especially when those things remind them of their kids.

Your Family

- How has technology already been a tool to show your teenagers you care?

- Which of these additional ideas might make your connections with your kids even stronger?

High School Bible

Wanting to show their sixteen-year-old son how much they cared about him, Pete and Kathy bought a Bible for him. But they didn't give it to him. They kept it themselves and used it for the next two years as their own devotional Bible. They prayed through it and made notes in it about passages that specifically related to their son. Then they presented it to him when he turned eighteen.

Pete and Kathy did the same for their other three children, starting when each turned sixteen. For all four of their young adult children, that Bible (even when it sits unopened on a bedroom shelf) is a powerful symbol of their parents' spiritual investment.

Your Family

- This two-year project takes a major commitment of time, energy, and prayer. For many of us, that commitment may seem beyond our capacity. What could you do, even for a few weeks or a month, that would help you share your spiritual insights with your teenagers?

If You Want to Be My Boyfriend, You Have to Meet My Dad

Mark had a simple policy with his two high school daughters: any guy who wanted to seriously date one of them had to meet with him first. Mark used the half hour coffee with the soon-to-be-boyfriend to talk with him about purity in dating and to let him know how precious his daughters are.

Mark's wife reflects, "I don't think any guy ever ran from our girls in fear. But I know that every guy knew Mark was an active father who was keeping an eye on his girls. Our girls knew that too."

Your Family

- What role, if any, have you played in your teenagers' dating relationships?

- Do you have any additional ideas that might be less potentially embarrassing to your kids and still show them how much you care?

Weekly Coffee Shop Meetings

Angel wanted to study a book about godliness with his seventeen-year-old son, but he wanted their discussions to feel special and manly. So instead of talking at home, Angel meets his son at a local coffee shop. Angel makes a point of not being home before their meetings so that his son has to meet him at the coffee house. In talking through each chapter, father and son answer questions like, What stood out to you about this chapter? What questions do you have? What difference might this chapter make in your life?

The urgent and unimportant will always intrude if you don't have a plan. If you come in my office, I have a master calendar. I put all mandatory meetings—meaning meetings my boss has scheduled—onto my calendar first. Next go my personal times with my wife and kids. Once I have my family time on my calendar, then I add the rest of my work appointments.

—Stuart

Angel's son loves meeting his dad at a coffee shop and being treated like a peer. Well, almost like a peer. Angel still buys both their drinks, which is a small price to pay for the weekly chats with his son.

Your Family

- How much one-on-one time do you get with your teenager?

- How would meeting your teenager at a nearby restaurant or coffee house bring a different dynamic to your time together?

- What other ideas can you think of to make your time with your teenager feel more adult?

Investing in Memories

Once Daniel became a dad, he committed to investing in building family memories. His gifts for his kids are generally something the family can enjoy together, like tickets to an amusement park or movie passes.

One Christmas, Daniel and his wife decided to get bikes for both of his kids. Now at least once a month, all four of them go on bike rides, often all-day trips lasting from morning to evening (with plenty of snack and meal stops along the way).

Riding bikes has deepened his relationships with his teenagers. As they pedal along streets and sidewalks, Daniel asks his kids questions they don't have time to discuss in the short bursts of time they have together at home or in the car. During one ride, Daniel asked his son, "What is one thing you wish I would do differently?"

His son thought for a few seconds and then answered, "Be nicer to Mom."

It was a turning point for Daniel, in both his relationship with his son and his relationship with his wife.

Your Family

- How do you already try to invest in family memories?
- As you think ahead to the next major holiday, what gifts could you give that would build family memories?

Family Scripture Passage

When their children entered high school, Paul and Corrina felt their family needed a Scripture passage as a "family mantra." Paul and Corrina hoped to find a passage that captured their hopes for their family, but they wanted the passage to be one that their children could easily embrace.

After brainstorming with their kids themes to include in their mantra, Paul and Corrina felt led to Paul's words in Romans 12:9–13: "Love must be sincere. Hate what is evil; cling to what is good. Be devoted to one another in love. Honor one another above yourselves. Never be lacking in zeal, but keep your spiritual fervor, serving the Lord. Be joyful in hope, patient in affliction, faithful in prayer. Share with the Lord's people who are in need. Practice hospitality."

Paul and Corrina hung this passage in their kitchen and gave both their kids a laminated copy of it. When their kids showed only moderate interest in the passage, Paul and Corrina wondered whether their kids viewed it as Mom and Dad's thing or their own thing. That question was answered when their fifteen-year-old mentioned she had hung the passage inside her locker at her public school.

During my interview with Paul, I asked him, "Do you think your family will ever adopt a new passage?"

He answered, "No way. Our kids won't let us."

Your Family

- What Scripture verses are meaningful to your teenagers?
- How can you make those verses a more central part of your home, family, and relationships?

Our Family's Steps toward Sticky Faith

Take a few moments on your own, or with your spouse, your friends, or your small group, to reflect on some potential next steps toward Sticky Faith.

Sticky Findings

On a scale of 1 to 5 (with 1 being "we stink at this" and 5 being "we rock at this"), rate your family on the research findings presented in this chapter.

1| I step into my kids' world instead of expecting them to step into mine.

① ② ③ ④ ⑤

2| I protect our family time together.

① ② ③ ④ ⑤

3| Our family has both planned and spontaneous time together.

① ② ③ ④ ⑤

4| I don't favor one of my children over the others.

① ② ③ ④ ⑤

Sticky Ideas

1| What are you already doing to spend time with your teenager in ways that are meaningful to them?

2| Given your ranking of the findings in the previous section, as well as the ideas you've read in this chapter, what one or two changes might you want to make in your family?

3| What can you do in the next few weeks or month to move toward these changes?

Chapter 6

Community

The Power of Five Faith-Building Adults

When Nathan turned thirteen, he didn't just have a birthday. He had a birth-month.

Dave and I wanted Nathan to know that as he officially became a teenager, he wasn't stepping through the hallway from childhood to adolescence alone. He had a team who walked through that passageway with him, cheering him on.

So two months before his birthday, Dave, Nathan, and I identified five men who were already influential in his life. We emailed each man, asking him if he'd be open to spending a few hours with Nathan during his birthday month. In addition to their using those hours to make a deposit into their relational account with Nathan, we also asked each to share with Nathan one piece of life advice and one piece of spiritual advice.

These men are busy fathers and grandfathers, but to our delight, each accepted. So five different men — ages thirty-seven to seventy-two — spent a few hours with Nathan that month. From golfing to a sunrise hike, these men shared memories, life stories, advice, and prayers. As Nathan recounted to Dave and me what he had learned from each man, we were filled with gratitude to God for these godly men who were pouring themselves into Nathan and our family.

To memorialize the time with these five men, Dave and Nathan built a wooden "team box" the size of a shoebox. In the box, we placed pictures of Nathan with each man, as well as a written copy of each man's spiritual and life advice. As God brings other amazing men across Nathan's path, we plan on asking them to spend some time with Nathan and adding their pictures and advice to Nathan's team box. The box now sits on Nathan's bookshelf, a palpable reminder of the amazing men who are already on Nathan's team, as well as those who we pray will join in future years.

Dave and I are not that creative. We never would have come up with this ritual that we've already done with Nathan—and plan to do with our two daughters as they turn thirteen—without the insights and ideas that emerged during our years of Sticky Faith research.

Sticky Findings

1 *The Power of Intergenerational Worship and Relationships*

When we launched our research, we were hoping to find a silver bullet that would lead to lasting faith in young people. We would have loved to uncover *the step* that every church or family could take to guarantee faith as the final destination.

The reality is that the journey toward Sticky Faith is too long and rocky to allow one step to be that determinative. Our team never found a silver bullet.

But we have found what we call "silver shavings." We studied the effects of thirteen different youth group participation variables, meaning thirteen various activities the typical church offers teenagers. You'll be glad to learn that service and short-term mission trips, small groups, student leadership, and retreats are important in building faith that lasts.

But the variable most correlated with mature faith in high school and college—the silver shavings of Sticky Faith—is involvement in intergenerational worship and relationships. In our study of five hundred youth group graduates, bringing the generations to sit shoulder-to-shoulder or look eye-to-eye was more important for long-term faith than any other youth group activity.

Bringing the generations together isn't a new idea, nor is it even our idea at the Fuller Youth Institute. Scripture is full of references to the power of God's activity through the generations, and how the generations need to declare examples of God's work to each other. It's impossible for us to "make [God's] faithfulness known through all generations" (Ps. 89:1) if our congregations are permanently divided into age-segregated classes, communities, and worship experiences.

2 While Intergenerational Connections Are Important, They Are Infrequent

As researchers, we weren't shocked when youth group kids who ranked five major sources of support (adults in the congregation, parents, youth workers, friends in youth group, and friends outside of youth group) listed adults in the congregation last.

What did surprise us was how far behind the other four groups they were.

One youth group graduate said that at her church, the adults seem to "see us as kind of scary because we're the people on the news who are dealing drugs and getting pregnant. They keep us separate and treat us like we are a hazard."

Even in times of personal struggle, young people are often adrift from adults in the church. Another study found that two-thirds of young adults who regularly attended a church or synagogue at the time of their parents' divorce report that no one—from either the clergy or the congregation—reached out to them.[1]

Outside of the faith community, young people similarly lack intergenerational anchors. According to research conducted by the Search Institute, only 45 percent of middle and high school students have three or more caring adults (outside of their parents) they can turn to for advice and support.[2]

3   Young People Benefit from at Least Five Supportive Adults

One study examining young adults who drop out of church found that 18 percent of youth group graduates who remain connected to the church had five or more adults invest in them spiritually and personally between ages fifteen and eighteen.[3]

That finding aligns with an astute recommendation made by our good friend and Fuller Seminary colleague Dr. Chap Clark. For the last few years, Chap has advocated that we need to "reverse the adult-to-kid ratio" in children's and youth ministries.

What does that mean? Many ministry leaders say they want to have one adult present for every five kids during small group meetings, Sunday school classes, or youth group activities. Chap's encouragement is to *reverse* that ratio so that instead of having one adult for every five kids, we have five adults for every one kid—5:1.

We're not talking about five Bible study leaders.

Nor are we talking about five adults to whom you outsource the spiritual, emotional, social, and intellectual development of your children.

We're talking about five adults who know your kids' names. Who pray for them. Who show up occasionally at your kids' gymnastics meets or volleyball tournaments. Five adults whom you have vetted as safe and caring people who can form a web of support to catch your kids when they stumble and fall.

The importance of surrounding young people with a team of caring adults is well captured in the term "social capital." The core idea of social capital is that social networks have value, increasing the productivity and well-being of individuals and groups. The value of social capital in the physical, emotional, mental, and spiritual health of children and teenagers has been well documented. In his widely acclaimed book *Bowling Alone*, Harvard University faculty member Robert D. Putnam summarizes, "Statistically, the correlation between high social capital and positive youth development is as close to perfect as social scientists ever find in data analyses of this sort."[4]

As parents, we can play a role in helping develop this support network for our kids. Having surveyed the research on children's social networks, Stanford University professor William Damon writes, "Parents do have the power to shape the forces that influence their children's development—more power than they may know, both within and beyond the confines of their own homes. The key to unleashing this power is to resist the isolation that has divided and confused households throughout our society."[5]

What if my child doesn't want to go to church or youth group? Should I make them go?

My answers to these questions have changed over the years. Previously I would have responded, "You should make them go. They need to know church is a priority."

That's still my general answer for parents of elementary and middle school children. My answer for high school students has become more nuanced.

What has changed? In addition to studying the steps to Sticky Faith described in this guide, I've also spent more time studying the ultimate nature of the church. The Greek word used by Paul in the New Testament for "church" is *ekklesia*, which is derived from two words: *ek*, meaning "from" or "out of," and *kaleo*, meaning "to call." For Paul, "the church" literally means "those who are called out of." He never meant a building; he always meant a group of people.

Given this understanding of "church" as a people and not a place, if your teenager resists attending church, you might try some of these suggestions:

Figure out why. Observe your child at youth group or around your church worship services. Talk with them about what they don't like about your church and what they wish were different. My experience is that about two-thirds of the time, teenagers don't like church because they don't feel they have friends there. They might say the teaching is boring or the worship music is lame, but if they had a close friend or two, they could stomach the rest.

Talk with your church's youth leader. As a youth leader, I appreciate hearing from parents when their child is struggling to fit in, because it makes me extra attentive to that child when they walk in our door. Brainstorm with your youth leader about who might be a good friendship fit for your child, and perhaps mention those students to your child.

Encourage your child to connect with

other kids who seem alone. If your child's disdain for church ultimately stems from their understandable fear that they will feel alone, encourage them to look for other kids who seem to sit or stand by themselves. Too many times, teenagers look at the clusters of kids who sit together, and conclude that everyone already has friends at youth group—not realizing that the perimeter of the room is full of single students like them.

Give your child a choice of attending one overnighter in the next six months. As I say in chapter 4, I've found that one overnighter or weekend away is the friendship-building equivalent to six months of attending Sunday youth group. Get the youth group calendar for the next six months and ask your child to choose one overnighter to attend. Consider consulting with your church's youth pastor about which trip is most likely to help your child grow social roots.

Offer a "youth group" alternative. As you've already learned in this chapter, there's far more to your student's long-term faith than attending youth group. Perhaps you could tell your teenager that they can skip youth group but need to regularly attend another Christ-centered community—such as a small group, your church's weekend worship services, or an on-campus parachurch ministry like Young Life, Youth for Christ, or Fellowship of Christian Athletes.

Connect them with a mentor. Some teenagers just don't jibe with youth ministry, no matter the flavor. Look for an adult your child already knows and trusts (or ask your youth pastor for any leads), and approach that person about meeting regularly with your teenager as a mentor. One-on-one discipleship might turn out to be something that keeps your son or daughter connected to the *ekklesia.*

Allow your child to attend a different church. If your teenager is drawn to a youth ministry at another church that is Christ-centered and vibrant, don't fight that momentum. Let them attend that youth group, either in addition to your church's or instead of it. You may even want to attend that church periodically to show your kids you want to walk with them through their faith-development journey.

4 The Church and Your Own Friends and Family <u>Are a Hotbed for Intergenerational Relationships</u>

Our team's interviews with fifty Sticky Faith parents revealed that one of the primary ways the church contributes to kids' faith is by providing intergenerational connections. Parents seemed more grateful for the church's role in creating intergenerational relationships — often through the youth group and the youth leaders — than for anything else the church provided for their kids, including Scripture study, prayer, worship, peer community, or other communal spiritual practices.

> When I turned sixteen, my parents moved away, but I wanted to finish high school, so I moved in with another family. After church and during the week, I would often go to the houses of other families at church and have so many good conversations. The adults at church became like my family.
>
> —Rachel

The five hundred youth group graduates we surveyed commonly reported that many of their strongest intergenerational connections were with their parents' friends or with extended family. The neighbor their mom walks with every Wednesday sent them emails in college, asking how she could be praying. Their uncle mailed a care package to their dorm room, complete with homemade brownies and a coffee gift card. It was often small gestures of care, taken by extended family or parents' friends, that made big impressions on young people.

That's good news for parents who wonder how to begin building a team of five adults for their kids. You likely need to look no farther than your close friends, family, and local church.

> Grandparents are often such key players in a family's intergenerational team that chapter 7 is entirely devoted to ideas for senior adults.

Sticky Ideas

Which Adults Do You Like?

One mom with teenage daughters has realized she doesn't have to keep her kids' 5:1 team a secret from them. Periodically she asks her daughters, "What adults do you like? Which of our relatives would you like to get to know better?" She mentally files away their answers so that when their family has free time for lunch after church on Sunday or her daughters face a tough championship softball game, she knows whom to invite along.

> *Our daughter has a couple of friends who have really amazing moms. These other moms have become our daughter's mentors. They pray for her and love her in ways that have been invaluable. These two women are very different from me, so she gets a different take on things from these wonderful women of faith.*
> —Marilyn

Another mom and dad with children in elementary school ask this same question and then use those adults as babysitters when needed.

Your Family

- If you were to ask your kids, "Which adults do you like?" who would you guess they would mention?
- Instead of guessing, when can you actually ask your kids that question?
- How can you involve those adults more in the life of your family?

5:1 Wallet Card

Barbara's nine-year-old daughter, Emma, was asked by her teacher to write a list of the five adults who were most important to her, outside of her parents. Pleased by this exercise, Barbara wanted this list to leave an indelible 5:1 mark on Emma.

First, Barbara asked Emma to place the names and phone numbers of those five people in Emma's wallet and in her school notebook so she'd always have them with her.

Second, Barbara encouraged Emma to call each of the five, letting them know that she had listed them for school and now carries around with her their names and phone numbers.

Imagine how it would feel to get that call from Emma, informing you that she had selected you as one of the five adults most important to her. The beauty of 5:1 is that it's powerful not only for the kids but also for the adults.

Because of our intergenerational covenant group, our kids grew up knowing they could call on any one of the adults for help. We met so much together that the adults understood who each kid was: their personality, friendships, spiritual growth, and painful moments. All of the kids in the group—many of whom are now adults—know beyond a shadow of a doubt we are there for them unconditionally.

—Ronaldo

Your Family

- What could you do to help your kids carry around with them the names and phone numbers of five adults?

- How would those five adults be encouraged if they knew how meaningful they were to your family?

Intergenerational Small Groups

A number of Sticky Faith families have developed intergenerational small groups to create a two-way street with other families. Not only do parents know that these adults have joined their kids' 5:1 team, but also they in turn get a green light to be part of other families' teams.

Various Sticky Faith parents have found the following helpful in their intergenerational small groups.

- Start with dinner together and some initial sharing over the meal. As the conversation deepens, allow younger children to peel off and head to another room.

- Take turns having each adult spend thirty to forty-five minutes (meaning basically the entire "content" of the meeting) sharing their spiritual autobiography, noting the people and experiences God has used to mold them.

- If meeting every other week, have an optional casual dinner together on alternate weeks. No one from the same family can sit next to each other at these dinners.
- Study books of the Bible together.
- Act out various passages of Scripture together.
- Share prayer requests and pray aloud for each other.
- Make sure to stay in touch between meetings, not only to share updates and prayer requests but also to invite other families to attend your kids' events. School plays, basketball tournaments, and Girl Scout ceremonies are all opportunities for small group members to show up and say (whether verbally or merely by their presence), "I'm part of your team."
- Capitalize on rhythms of the year, such as birthdays, the start of the school year, or the start of the calendar year, to allow group members to share and pray about fears, goals, and dreams.

Our research motivated our family to start our own intergenerational small group. Five years ago we invited a family in our life stage, a family ten years younger and still having babies, and a couple in their seventies to form a small group with our family. While Dave and I have each had plenty of small group experiences, they've always been with people in our life stage (and often of our own gender). Those past small groups have been great, but this intergenerational small group trumps them all. We've walked through everything from kindergarten to retirement together, and it has felt so right for all of us—from our youngest group member, at age two, to our oldest, at age seventy-three—to journey through those experiences with people from different generations.

> I'm a stay-at-home mom, and I'm part of a group of women who started meeting more than twenty years ago every Wednesday when our kids were little. We are still meeting together. These women are my soul sisters. My kids know that those friends have their best interest at heart and are praying for them. Other people often say, "I'm praying for you," but a lot of them don't really mean it. My kids know these women mean it.
>
> —Leigh

When we started meeting, we let the kids choose the name for the group. They chose Viper. So I'm a forty-four-year-old whose primary small group is called Viper.

Your Family

- If you're currently part of a small group, how do the members of that group already invest in your kids?

- How could the folks in that small group play a greater role in your kids' lives? What could you do to be part of the 5:1 team for the kids in another member's family?

- If you're not part of a small group, what would it look like for you to start an intergenerational small group? How would that type of small group benefit you and your kids?

 ## Path to Manhood

Ken wanted Danny's sixteenth birthday to be about more than cake, balloons, or even a driver's license. Ken wanted Danny to understand that he was now walking the path to manhood.

So Ken handpicked ten of his male friends and relatives who modeled godly characteristics that he hoped Danny would emulate. Ken asked each man to write down specific advice for Danny about that characteristic, including Scripture verses that had helped him develop that quality.

One Saturday morning, Ken invited Danny to take a walk around a lake. He explained that this particular walk represented Danny's journey into manhood. Interspersed around the lake were Ken's ten friends and family members. As Ken and Danny made their way around the lake, each of the ten joined them to share what they had written and to pray for Danny.

Not only does Danny now have a written copy of that tenfold advice, but also he knows ten men who are willing to continue walking with him as he journeys into adulthood.

Your Family

- Which birthday(s) do you consider especially important to highlight as your kids mature?
- How could you involve members of your kids' 5:1 team in those birthdays?

5:1 Journal

Julio had always wanted to walk with his son, Alberto, through some sort of literal path to manhood, but somehow he was never able to make it happen. So he came up with a different—yet equally powerful—idea that better fit his family.

Prior to Alberto's eighteenth birthday, Julio gave a number of Alberto's mentors a small sheet of paper, asking them to write down what they appreciated about Alberto and any advice they wanted to share with him. So Alberto's music teacher wrote about the importance of discipline, his youth pastor nudged Alberto toward purity in dating, the tech guy at their church encouraged Alberto to periodically unplug from technology, and Alberto's grandmother described the lessons she hoped he had learned from all the years they played Scrabble, alternating between English and Spanish. Julio collected those papers and compiled them (along with some pictures) in a special leather-bound journal as a birthday gift for Alberto. Alberto is very grateful that his dad went to the trouble of creating the journal, and Julio is very grateful to God for the friends and family who are part of his son's team.

> When our kids were teenagers, we reached out to our neighborhood and started a Bible study. Looking back, we should have integrated our kids more into that study. They observed, but they weren't really a part of those relationships.
>
> —Benson

Your Family

- What adults are already significantly shaping your child?
- What would it mean to your child to receive written advice and notes of appreciation from those adults?

Dads' Camping

Glyn's wife was more of a hotel person than a camping person. Since Glyn wanted to expose his kids to the fine art of camping, he invited a few other dads and their kids to spend a weekend at a campsite about forty-five minutes away from where they lived.

That was four years ago, and every year since then the trip has grown, both in quantity and in impact. Last spring, seven dads (including Glyn's brother-in-law) and their twenty-two kids went away for a forty-eight-hour camping trip together. As they took hikes, swam at a nearby beach, cooked over an open fire, and roasted marshmallows, dads and kids cross-pollinated. While these families are all part of the same church, the two days give the men and kids exponentially more opportunities to laugh and talk (as well as play practical jokes) than does the typical Sunday at church.

In case you're wondering, none of the moms has yet to complain about their annual weekend alone.

Your Family

- What opportunities do your kids already have to get to know other adults through weekend or weeklong trips?

- Whether or not you're a camping person, what type of overnighters with other families would fit your family habits and schedule?

Science Fair Project Bonding

Tina was a single parent whose eighth-grade daughter, Lauren, had to do a project for her school's science expo. Lauren decided to focus on roller coasters but was intimidated at the prospect of building a model of a local roller coaster. Tina shared this dilemma with her small group, and one of the senior adults in the group who had a background in carpentry volunteered to work with Lauren.

The rest of the small group chipped in to supply the wood, tools, and paint needed. By the end, the roller coaster was quite a masterpiece. It was so large and elaborate that Lauren had to keep measuring it to make sure it would fit through the front door of their apartment.

Because the small group was so invested in Lauren's roller coaster, they wanted to come to the science expo. The school had limited the number of tickets per student, so Lauren had to get special permission for that many guests. As Lauren explained to her teacher, "This is my small group, they want to be there, and I'd like them to be there."

Fifteen Ways to Show Kids (Yours and Others') That You Care

1. Ask them about school.

2. Find out their extracurricular activity schedule and go to at least one game, recital, or show.

3. Call them and sing to them on their birthday.

4. Swing by their house with ice cream after they've had a spectacular day.

5. Swing by their house with ice cream after they've had a lousy day.

6. Keep your promises, no matter how small.

7. Text them and share your three favorite things about them.

8. Find out their favorite candy and give it to them for no reason at all.

9. Give them your undivided attention.

10. Ask them how you can be praying for them. And then pray.

11. A week after you asked them how you can be praying for them, loop back and find out how they're doing.

12. Learn their top hobbies or interests and then connect them with someone you know who can teach them more about what's special to them.

13. Let them choose the music in the car, and learn why they lean toward that style.

14. Send them something—anything—in the mail.

15. Give them your phone number and let them know they can call you at any time, whether they need help or just to talk.

Your Family

- School projects can easily make not just kids but also parents feel like they are drowning in deadlines and poster board. What adults (maybe even retired adults) could step in and throw your family a lifeline?

- How would partnering with other adults in school projects strengthen the team of Sticky Faith adults surrounding your family?

 ## Parent-Teacher Conferences at Your Church

Just about every school in the US hosts annual or semiannual parent-teacher conferences. Parent-teacher conferences provide both sides with an opportunity to communicate and to develop a customized plan to help each individual child.

Inspired by your local school, you can try requesting a parent-teacher conference with your child's Sunday school teacher, small group leader, or pastor. When you do so, explain that your goal is to strengthen your family's connection with that teacher because you view them as an important part of your family's team.

You might want to send a few questions to that teacher ahead of time so that they can be prepared. Some possible questions include:

- What do you hope will happen this year in the class or group?

- What unique strengths or challenges does my child seem to have?

- What insights about God seem to most connect with my child?

- What teachings of Scripture do you think I should try to emphasize with my son or daughter?

- How does my child connect with others in the group?

- How can I best support what you do in the class?

As much as possible, communicate your warm and enthusiastic support for your child's teacher or pastor. Odds are good that they are volunteering their time to be with your child, so let them know that you want to be their biggest cheerleader. In fact, ask how you can be praying for them, and then pray aloud for them at the end of your conference.

Your Family

- What leaders at your church are closest to your child?
- Whether it be through a parent-teacher conference or a less structured conversation, how can you strengthen those leaders' connection with your family and your child?

 ## Kid Swaps

Many Sticky Faith parents have found that "swapping kids" with another family is a fun and memorable way to surround their kids with a 5:1 team. Some families join forces and take turns having all the kids over to their house for the evening. For instance, one set of parents we interviewed coordinates a monthly "parents' night out" with the other four families in their small group. The five families take turns hosting all the kids at one house for an evening. So each month, the host couple dives into an evening of chaotic fun with all those kids while the rest of the couples gain a precious date night.

A few families we met during the course of our research take a more literal approach to kid swapping. They actually exchange kids for the night. The kids know they'll be having dinner and doing something fun with another set of parents, but the remaining details of the evening are a surprise. Kids and adults go miniature golfing, complete scavenger hunts in local malls, or cook an elaborate dinner—all activities meant to help parents build relationships with their "new" kids.

Two families created an Uber-Extreme-Kids-Swap. They exchange kids for an entire week. Usually these weeks are over the summer, so homework is not a factor. But sports, camps, and kids' plans with friends are all part of the new family's juggling act.

No, this weeklong kids swap is not a reality TV show. It is two families' plan to move from rhetoric to reality with their 5:1 teams.

Your Family

- Whether you're thinking it would be an hour or a week, what might a kid swap look like for your family?
- What would you gain by such a swap?
- Let's be honest: there is a cost to these sorts of kid swaps (exhaustion, confusion, disruption of habits). So what might you also lose?

Our Family's Steps toward Sticky Faith

Take a few moments on your own, or with your spouse, your friends, or your small group, to reflect on some potential next steps toward Sticky Faith.

Sticky Findings

On a scale of 1 to 5 (with 1 being "we stink at this" and 5 being "we rock at this"), rate your family on the research findings presented in this chapter.

1| My kids have at least five adults who are on their team.

① ② ③ ④ ⑤

2| My friends, extended family, and church know and support our kids.

① ② ③ ④ ⑤

3| I am investing in kids in other families.

① ② ③ ④ ⑤

Sticky Ideas

1| What are you already doing to connect your kids with a web of caring adults?

2| Given your ranking of the findings in the previous section, as well as the ideas you've read in this chapter, what one or two changes might you want to make in your family?

3| What can you do in the next few weeks or month to move toward these changes?

Chapter 7

Grandparents and Senior Adults
The Magic of Intergenerational Interaction

Every kid needs a Ruth.

Every family needs a Ruth.

Every church needs a Ruth.

Even though I spent only a few minutes with Ruth, she permanently colored my picture of senior adults' impact in faith-pursuing families.

Ruth wore thick glasses and appeared to be in her late eighties. After hearing me present our research about Sticky Faith families at an evening church seminar, she approached me as I was putting away my laptop, to share her own strategy for helping students stay connected with God.

Ruth explained, "At the start of every fall, I ask our church for a list of the high school seniors who have just graduated. I get those students' names and addresses, and I write them all letters to let them know I'm thinking of them and praying for them. I tell them they don't have to write me back, and most don't. But when they come home at Thanksgiving or Christmas, they thank me for writing them."

As I drove away from the host church, I couldn't stop thinking about Ruth. Her willingness to put pen to paper to write each student one letter at the start of every fall was inspiring.

The next day, I felt prompted to share about Ruth as I was teaching our Sticky Faith research in the same city but to a different audience. Or as I was about to find out, to a mostly different audience.

After I described Ruth and her amazing commitment to write one letter at the start of every fall to each high school graduate, an audience member raised his hand. I called on him, and he stood to explain, "I was here last night and saw Ruth talking to you. I know Ruth. We're part of the same church. She doesn't write those high school graduates once at the start of every fall. She writes them *every* week."

Maybe you're thinking what I and many audience members said aloud that day: *Wow*.

Ruth reminds us that there's a group of people with untapped potential to don a jersey and join your family's Sticky Faith team.

Senior adults.

Grandparents. Some are biological grandparents, meaning they are related to your kids. Others are adopted, or "functional," grandparents, meaning they are not genetically related to your family but play the same role and relate to your kids like grandparents.[1]

A grandmother herself, Ruth wasn't satisfied with merely nurturing her own family tree. She branched out to encourage other young people. Ruth had prayed that God would send caring adults into her grandkids' lives. She decided that she would be an answer to those very same prayers of other grandparents.

> I had no grandparents growing up, but I've always had a special love for older people. When a woman in her late eighties needed a ride home from church each week, I started giving her a ride. This wonderful woman never had any kids or grandkids of her own, so she ended up pretty much adopting ours. We started visiting her at her house, and she ended up teaching my daughter how to sew and make her own doll clothes. When she died at age 107, it was a huge loss for our entire family.
>
> —Monique

If you're a grandparent, I hope these findings and ideas help you pour faith into your own grandchildren. I pray that the story of Ruth inspires you to channel your faith toward other children and teenagers as well.

If you're a parent who can recruit your own parents and in-laws to be part of your family's team, you might want to share some of this chapter's suggestions with them. If you're a parent without the support of extended family, odds are good there's a Ruth in your neighborhood or congregation who would be honored to help you encircle your kids with the love and support they need.

Sticky Findings

1 *Grandparents Are More Involved Than Ever*

The data supports what you may have noticed as you've looked at who is picking up kids after school: grandparents are more engaged than in previous generations.

According to gerontologist Dr. Vern Bengtson from the University of Southern California, the following factors are contributing to this increase in grandparents' engagement.

- Senior adults' health is improving, and their life expectancy is increasing.
- As more and more families have two parents who work outside of the home, grandparents are providing more after-school care.
- Grandparents have new ways to connect with their grandchildren through technology like Skype, Facebook, and text messaging.

As a result of these and other cultural factors, Bengtson and his team surmise that "Gen Xers and Millennials will have greater involvement with their grandparents—and, for some, their great-grandparents—than any previous generation of grandchildren in American history."[2]

2 *Involvement = Influence*

The question grandparents ask our team most frequently is, My kids are part of the 40–50 percent who have drifted from the faith. Can I still have an influence on my grandkids?

Research says yes!

When it comes to religious influence on grandchildren, grandparents tend to choose one of four paths:

1. Grandparents can reinforce the parents' religious influence.
2. Grandparents can substitute for the parents' influence.

3. Grandparents can subvert the parents' influence.

4. Grandparents can ignore religion.[3]

Especially in the first three cases, grandparents have a significant influence on their grandkids' faith, and not just when grandparents align with parents' faith (as in the first path). Even when researchers statistically control for parents' faith influence, grandparents have a separate and independent impact on grandkids' faith.[4]

The data doesn't tell *why* grandparents have such influence. It might be they often have more time and focus to invest in kids' faith development than do busy and preoccupied parents. Or perhaps grandparents are simply more immune to conflict with teenagers than parents are.

Whatever the reason, it's good news if the senior adults in your kids' lives are passionate about their relationship with Christ. It's not-so-good news to those of you whose children are around senior adults who may (even unintentionally) be undermining your Sticky Faith plans.

What if my child's grandparents influence them in ways I wish they didn't?

Extra electronics and extra sugar. In my opinion, a few ounces of spoiling are a grandparent's role, if not right.

But if your concerns expand beyond an occasional additional half hour of video games or a once-in-a-while second bowl of ice cream, you might consider the following:

Talk to the grandparents by starting with the positive. Always. No matter who I'm giving input to, I always try to start by affirming what they are doing well. Begin the conversation by thanking your parents or in-laws for who they are and how they are investing in your kids. Give them specific examples of what you appreciate about how they support your family and shape your child.

Pick the right battles. You might have ten items you wish the grandparents would do differently, but that's eight items too many. Choose one or two as a focus for your conversation.

Emphasize what's best for your child.
You might try pointing out how staying up late all weekend can sabotage your child at school the next week. Or that bouncing back and forth from your family's regular rules to grandparent evenings without boundaries is confusing for your kid. The reality is, you're ultimately motivated by what's best for your child, so approach the conversation with that as the goal.

Give the grandparents a short article that explains your parenting strategy.
If having a discussion with your parents or in-laws seems fraught with conversational land mines, let someone else share the message through an article or blog post.

If they are in some way hurting your child, separate them from your child.
If a grandparent's constant criticism or lack of attentiveness is potentially hurtful to your child, your priority is your child. Do what you have to do in order to prevent your child from absorbing messages that can damage their view of themselves and the world around them. If you suspect any form of abuse, separate your child immediately and consider whether outside authorities should be involved.

---

3 ## Closer to God = Closer to Your Grandkids

Across faith traditions, grandparents who are highly religious have stronger relationships with their grandchildren and are more involved in their lives.[5] Given the previous finding about the power of grandparent involvement, that's an asset if the "highly religious" grandparent has dedicated their life to Christ. It can be a liability if the "highly religious" grandparent would rather nudge your kids away from Jesus and down a different faith path.

> Watching our boys observe their grandfather care for their grandmother in the ten years that Alzheimer's was part of her life was amazing. They saw him be Christ in action.
> —Alec

Sticky Ideas

This chapter is unlike the rest, for two reasons. First, most of the ideas for grandparents emerge not from our multiyear Sticky Faith study or from our fifty interviews with Sticky Faith parents. Instead they come from grandparents who are part of the Fuller Youth Institute community and who have used our research as a springboard to dive into deeper relationships with their grandkids.

Second, thanks to these amazing senior adults, we've discovered so many wonderful ideas that it was hard to sift through them and choose the best. So we opted to describe more "rapid-fire" ideas —in less detail and with fewer "Your Family" questions—than in any other chapter. If you are a senior adult, we hope you'll dig through these insights and unearth the treasure that helps you connect to your grandkids or other children special to you. If you are a parent, you might look for one or two ideas to pass along to your parents, your in-laws, or another senior adult to encourage their relationship with your children. At the end of the chapter, we'll ask each of you—grandparent or parent—to rate your effectiveness in this area of faith-building in your children and grandchildren.

 ## Ideas That Can Be Done Any Day, at Any Time

- Start a book club with your grandkids. Invite them to keep a list of books that they've read (or that someone has read to them). Set a goal with them, and after they read the predetermined number of books, reward them with a small prize or special outing. Or perhaps you and your grandchild can agree to read the same book and then meet to discuss it over a treat.

- Take a few hours to teach your grandchildren about being mindful. As you eat together, talk about where your food comes from and who was involved with growing, transporting, and even selling the items. Take a walk in your neighborhood together, making an effort to be mindful of what you see, hear, and smell. When you are struck by something beautiful, thank God aloud for it.

- Since grandparents are often important bridges to children's family heritage, teach your grandchildren about their culture. Enjoy your favorite cultural art, dress, and customs together as an extended family. Help your grandchildren learn how to make specific cultural foods, or visit places in your community that have a poignant meaning or connection to your family background.

- Invite your grandchildren for sleepovers at your house. While they are over, engage in some of their favorite activities together. (Try to carve out time the next day so you can take a nap.)

- Don't just pray *for* your grandkids; pray *with* them also. As you pray, thank God aloud for the special qualities he has given them.

- Create a drama of a Bible story with your grandkids. Act it out whether or not you have an audience.

- Have a talent show together. Adults and children can participate. No act is too small!

My wife's dad was pretty uninvolved in her life when she was a teenager. But he's like a different man with our son. He even takes him every year to a major music festival where they camp and listen to lots of rock 'n' roll. As weird as it is that our son's grandfather takes him to this festival, our son is never, ever going to forget it. Our son might even someday take his own grandson to a festival.

—Anders

- Write a prayer of blessing for your grandchildren, noting Scripture verses that you long to be true in their lives, both now and in the future. Keep a copy for yourself and give copies (maybe even framed) to your grandkids to remind them that they have a grandparent who is praying for them.

- Teach your grandchild a new skill or share one of your favorite hobbies with them, such as fishing, skiing, bicycling, or making jewelry.

- Let your grandchild teach *you* a new skill or share a hobby with you.

- Purchase or create a craft or science project that you can do with your grandchild.

- Enter a race and run, swim, ride, or walk it with your grandchild.

- Talk with your grandchild about a family tradition that you enjoyed with your own grandparents or parents and have passed along to your children. Then continue that tradition with your grandchild. Examples could include seeing fireworks together or going to a summer parade, having campfires and roasting marshmallows on the beach, seeing the *Nutcracker* ballet or making tamales during the Christmas season, or riding bikes to a favorite ice cream shop.

- Bring out photo albums and talk about when your grandchild was born, how you prayed for them even before they were born, how excited you were to first hold them, and how blessed you feel that they are now part of your family.

- Serve together at a local ministry.

- Feed homeless folks in your community.

- Play games together.

- Teach your grandchildren to sing, and enjoy singing with them. In the car, play a singing game by having each person take a turn humming a tune of a song you all know. The one who identifies that song gets to hum the next one.

- Plant flowers or a tree with your grandchild. Commemorate occasions (whether celebrations or challenging times) by planting special trees or plants. When you and your grandkids see those plants in the future, it will give you a chance to share about God's presence in the highs and lows of life.

- Cook with your grandchildren. While in the kitchen, play music and sing or even dance together.

- Build something with your grandchildren.

- Share times when you have blown it, or when you have disobeyed what you sensed God was telling you to do. Let your grandchildren know how glad you are that Jesus forgives you no matter what.

Ideas for Grandparents Who Live Farther Away

- Choose a book series to read with your grandchildren. Read to them using the phone or a videoconference service. As they get older and the books get longer, read separately and then use technology to discuss the book's highlights together.

- Write letters to your grandkids, telling them how much you love them, what you specifically love about them, and what gifts you see in them. Tell them how thankful you are that God has made them so special.

- Have breakfast together once a week using the phone or a videoconference service.

- Start a collection of something with your grandchild, such as dolls from other countries, interesting stones, matchbooks, coins, or colored glass. Continue adding to the collection when you travel or when you are together.

- Text them on an ordinary day and let them know you're thinking about them.

- Pray for your grandkids, and tell them the specific things you are asking God to do for them or show them.

- Send packages! Especially at holidays and birthdays when you are apart, packages with even small, inexpensive gifts or treats are memorable to kids. When they move away from home, send an occasional package to school with homemade cookies or a gift card to a coffee shop.

- Call or send a letter when kids have special events or milestones at school or church. For instance, while you may not be present for a baptism, calling your grandchild on that special day is still very memorable. The same can be true of soccer tournaments, school plays, or after a church retreat weekend.

- If financially possible, offer to pay travel expenses so your grandchild can come stay with you for a long weekend or more, without siblings or parents.

Ideas Involving Vacations or Extended Time Together

- Before your grandkids come for a visit, ask them some questions so you know what they want to do, such as, What do you want to do with Grandpa? How about with Grandma? What food would you like to eat? What places do you want to visit? What movie would you like to see? Where do you want to go with your cousins?

- On extended-family vacations, try to have morning or evening devotions that include questions that all family members can answer. This way, the children hear their parents, grandparents, aunts, uncles, and cousins share on a deeper level.

- When your grandchild reaches the age of twelve or thirteen, take them on a weekend away with other significant adults of the same gender in your family, including their mom or dad and aunts or uncles. Have a planned activity that you do together (like skiing, hiking, going to a Broadway show, or camping). Include time to discuss what it means to be a Christian man or woman. Give your grandchild a lasting memento that will remind them of what they learned and committed to over the weekend.

- Host "Camp Grandparents" with your grandkids, either at your house or at another destination. Do things together that they would do at camp, such as crafts, sports, singing, cooking, and treasure hunts. This could last one day or several days. Or enroll them in a local half-day summer camp, then spend the other half of the day doing activities together. Local colleges, museums, and recreation centers often offer camps covering a wide variety of interests, such as art, science, computers, athletics, music, and nature, so be sure to check with your grandchild to find out what interests them. Or find a camp or campground that caters to family activities, and let that organization plan the programming and details.

- Go on a mission trip with your grandchild, either locally or abroad. Consider making this a rite-of-passage experience that you share with each grandchild as they reach a certain age.

- If possible, pay for your grandchild to attend a church camp and have them share about it with you afterward.

A Parent's Steps toward Sticky Faith

If you are a parent, take a few moments on your own, or with your spouse, your friends, or your small group, to reflect on some potential next steps toward Sticky Faith.

Sticky Findings

On a scale of 1 to 5 (with 1 being "we stink at this" and 5 being "we rock at this"), rate your family on the research findings presented in this chapter.

1| My kids have close relationships with senior adults, whether they be biological or functional grandparents.

① ② ③ ④ ⑤

2| I feel good about the faith commitment and influence of these grandparents.

① ② ③ ④ ⑤

Sticky Ideas

1| In what ways are senior adults already helping to instill Sticky Faith in your kids?

2| Given your ranking of the findings in the previous section, as well as the ideas you've read in this chapter, what one or two changes might you want to make in your family?

3| What can you do in the next few weeks or month to move toward these changes?

A Grandparent's Steps toward Sticky Faith

If you are a grandparent, take a few moments on your own, or with your spouse, your friends, or your small group, to reflect on how you can nudge your grandchildren, or other children you care about, toward a faith that lasts.

Sticky Findings

On a scale of 1 to 5 (with 1 being "I stink at this" and 5 being "I rock at this"), rate yourself on the research findings presented in this chapter.

1| I have a close relationship with my grandkids.

① ② ③ ④ ⑤

2| My grandkids know about my faith.

① ② ③ ④ ⑤

3| I talk with my grandkids about my faith.

① ② ③ ④ ⑤

4| I regularly show my grandkids I care about them.

① ② ③ ④ ⑤

Sticky Ideas

1| In what ways are you already helping to build into your grandkids a faith that lasts?

2| Given your ranking of the findings in the previous section, as well as the ideas you've read in this chapter, what one or two changes might you want to make in the way you relate to your grandchildren and to other children in your life?

3| What can you do in the next few weeks or month to move toward these changes?

Chapter 8

Communication

Talking Faith with Your Kids

Thirteen-year-old Steve attended a local church most weekends with his parents. As a bright and curious sixth-grader, Steve was fine going to church with his family but hadn't committed his life to Christ. He had far too many unanswered questions about God.

One Sunday after church, Steve asked his senior pastor one of those questions. "Pastor, if I raise my finger, will God know which one I'm going to raise even before I raise it?"

The pastor replied, "Yes. God knows everything."

Steve, who was especially troubled by children who were starving in Africa, then pulled out a *Life* magazine cover depicting hungry African children and asked the logical follow-up. "Well, does God know about this and what's going to happen to those children?"

A tougher question, to be sure, but the pastor gave a similar response. "Steve, I know you don't understand, but yes, God knows about that."[1]

Steve walked out of church that day and never again returned to a Christian church. There was nothing technically wrong with the pastor's answer, but if God knew what was happening in Africa and didn't stop it, Steve wanted nothing to do with God.

You've likely heard of this Steve.

His last name is Jobs.

Yes, the Steve Jobs who was the cofounder, CEO, and chair of Apple.

Yes, the Steve Jobs who was the charismatic pioneer of the personal computer revolution and shepherded the development of the iMac, iPhone, iPod, iPad, and iTunes.

That Steve Jobs was a churchgoing junior high student who had questions about faith. There is no record of him discussing these questions or his faith with his parents. When he tried to talk with his pastor, the pastor's answer—although well intentioned—repelled Steve from the faith.

Steve Jobs had an unquestionable impact on our technology; because of his work, we interact with the world and each other differently. In the field of technology, he didn't just usher in a new chapter; he launched a whole new book series.

But imagine if Steve had been greeted by a different answer from his pastor. One that was less of a conversational dead end and more of an on-ramp to a deeper discussion about faith.

Imagine if the pastor had replied to thirteen-year-old Steve, "That's a great question, Steve. How about if you and I and your dad meet for breakfast this week and talk about it?"

Imagine if an adult had hit the conversational ball over the net to Steve, instead of letting it slowly roll off the court.

Imagine if Steve's questions were answered by his parents or pastor, and he poured his entrepreneurial brilliance not just into furthering high-tech interfaces but also into furthering the gospel. Imagine what our world might be like if Steve had funneled his leadership resources into both Silicon Valley and God's kingdom.

I believe our world would be different. The world your kids will experience during their lifetime would be different.

Unfortunately, there's no record of any adult having those conversations with Steve. So I still have a great Apple computer, but I wistfully wonder what might have been, not just for Steve but for all of us.

Sticky Findings

1 ## Ask Questions, but Share Your Own Story Too

If you're like most parents, your typical "dialogue" with your child about faith consists of your asking them questions, generally after church.

"How was church today?"

"What did you learn?"

"What passage of Scripture did you study?"

Depending on your child's mood, personality, and relationship with you, you might get a few sentences in return. But usually the answers are more brief.

"Fine."

"Not much."

"I forgot."

And sometimes you get even less, like just a grunt or a "leave me alone" eye roll.

Our data of more than five hundred youth group graduates suggests that these questions can pay off. So keep asking them. But just as important is that you share about your own faith too. Don't just interview your kids; also share organically and authentically about your own spiritual pilgrimage.

When he was in high school, our son had a problem with pornography. We limited his access to the internet, and that helped. But equally important were the conversations he and I had together. I was truthful with him and told him I had had problems with pornography also.

—Marvin

The picture that emerges from our research mirrors that presented by the Lord in Deuteronomy 6:7. Parents are to share about faith "when you sit at home and when you walk along the road, when you lie down and when you get up." In other words, as much as we can, whenever we have a chance.

But please don't give your kids a lecture. Or lots of lectures. Instead look for opportunities to organically share a few sentences or paragraphs about what you're learning in church, what you're praying about, or new lessons God is showing you about life or parenthood.

As you have perhaps experienced, this type of open conversation is often more challenging as kids get older. One nationwide study of positive family communication reveals a significant difference between the families of middle school students and those of high school students. While 47 percent of sixth-graders report having positive communication in their families, that number drops to 22 percent by the end of high school.[2]

2 Doubt Is Most Toxic When It Goes Unexpressed

While parents often worry that their kids' doubts are wrong or sinful, our research brings a counterperspective. In our study of five hundred students, we found that young people who feel the freedom and have the opportunity to express their doubt have greater faith maturity than those who don't.

So doubt in and of itself isn't necessarily dangerous. It's *unexpressed* doubt that is most toxic. Unfortunately, less than half of the students we interviewed have shared their doubts and struggles with an adult or a friend.

When we asked youth group graduates to name their most pressing doubts, they gave us a wide variety of answers, ranging from, Is homosexuality that bad? to Will non-Christians really go to hell? Yet in the midst of their diverse doubts, the most common doubts tended to be (listed in no particular order):

- Does God exist?
- Is Christianity true and the only way to God?
- Does God love me?
- Am I living the life God wants?

Interestingly, the first two questions are classic apologetics questions. The last two are more personal and more directly related to the student's life. The message to parents is that we need to provide a time and place for our young people to grapple with both types of questions.

Adolescence isn't the only stage when these four questions are raised. The chorus of folks asking these questions begins in elementary school and ends in the retirement center. Given the previous finding, the good news is that when we parents share that we have wondered about these same questions, God might open a door for candid conversations with our kids about some of their doubts too.

3 Ironically, Christian Parents Are Less Likely to Talk about Tricky Subjects with Their Kids

Perhaps our kids stay silent because we parents are too afraid or too busy to talk about tough subjects like doubt. Many of us have a mental list of topics we hope we can avoid discussing with our kids.

Sex is certainly on that list. According to two different sets of data, the more important that religion (including Christianity) is to parents, the more difficult it is for those parents to talk with their kids about sex.[3]

I find that both sad and ironic. We followers of Christ should

---

What if my kid rolls their eyes and sighs when I bring up God?

Maybe it's your kid's personality. Perhaps it's the emotional canyon that has grown between you. Or possibly it's just your kid's mood this month.

Whatever the reason, if your kids don't want to dive into conversations with you about God, that's okay. It may not be ideal, but it's normal. You probably didn't want to talk with your parents about your every emotional and spiritual question.

Your goal is that your child talk to an adult who is a Christ follower, even if it's not you.

Discuss with your child who they might want to talk to. It could be someone at your church or a family member in another city whom they could visit or talk to by phone or webcam. Prep that person ahead of time by letting them know what you perceive in your child. If appropriate, connect with that adult afterward (without snooping for details) so you can partner with them in your child's spiritual growth through prayer and other "behind the scenes" roles.

be at the front of the line to talk with our kids about sex, because we know that sex, when done right, is really right. Somehow with sex (as well as other controversial topics), our families have been robbed of healthy, balanced, scripturally guided conversations, the type of conversations that foster Sticky Faith.

4 The Best Conversations Are Inspired by Life

Many of the Sticky Faith parents we interviewed had structured family conversations and Bible studies, especially when their kids were in elementary school. Yet those same parents often commented that their best discussions were triggered by life, not by a schedule.

Like when a daughter was getting hurtful texts late at night.

Or when a son was wondering if he should join the military after graduation.

Or when a stepson was unsure about his girlfriend's commitment to him.

As one dad explained, "Often if I just start talking to them about faith, they have a tendency to put up a wall. Our discussions are much better when they start with something they're experiencing and then move into how God relates to that area."

Sometimes at meals we will read a devotional and pray together. If it's a chaotic day and our kids erupt in a concert of burps while we're trying to read together, we know it's not going to be one of those great mealtime conversations, and we just move on.

—Lois

This interview theme is confirmed by another recent study of parents and teenagers in highly religious Christian, Jewish, and Muslim families. While various techniques were acknowledged as important in shaping kids' faith (including family devotions and family worship times), parents and adolescents both cited faith conversations more than any other method (these conversations were named by more than 75 percent of each group) as being vital to molding faith. In particular, *youth-centered* conversations, meaning those that focus on teenagers' issues and concerns, were identified as the best catalysts for deepening faith.[4]

5 If Conversations Are Win-Lose, Parents Have Already Lost

As you might have guessed, your kids aren't hoping that the result of any family discussion is that they will end up agreeing with you. Not only do they not want that; they might push against you and your faith if you try to make it happen.

The goal of your conversations isn't to verbally arm wrestle your child into submission. Many students with lasting faith appreciate the freedom their parents have always given them to arrive at their own opinions and decisions. One student described the "incredible conversations" he has had with his parents over the years, "where we're learning from each other. They share with me why they believe what they believe, and then they let me share what I believe. It feels like an opportunity for growth for both my parents and me."

6 Moms' Special Role in Faith Conversations

While faith discussions with both parents are important, if we wanted to compare the impact of mothers and fathers, moms might nose ahead.

In a large study of religiously diverse adolescents, researchers observed differences in the roles of mothers and fathers. The study confirmed what we presented in chapter 4: fathers' general care and concern for kids makes more of a difference in long-term faith than does that of mothers. But when it comes to faith conversations in particular, moms seem to trump. Teenagers' spirituality was more related to their mothers' spiritual support and dialogue than to their fathers'.[5]

> I was told by both of our kids that I just didn't know when to let something go and that I intruded too much. So I tried not to be the "answer gal" for my kids. I tried to listen for the tiny little cues that they were open to talking. But it was so hard.
>
> —Evie

That doesn't mean that fathers are unimportant. Let's be clear: dads are vital conversation partners with their kids. But as significant as dads are, when it comes to diving into faith conversations, moms' impact is perhaps a few feet deeper.

Sticky Ideas

 ## Wow, Pow, Holy Cow, How

Every night at dinner, the Smithson family discusses four topics related to their day: *Wow, Pow, Holy Cow, How.*

Wow is the best part of their day.

Pow is the worst part of their day.

Holy Cow is something in their day that pointed them to God.

How is an opportunity in their day to be the answer to someone else's prayer.

As family members share their experiences for each topic, the Smithsons discuss everything from softball tournaments and science tests to sales presentations and software design. To prevent things from feeling too fake or forced, family members are allowed to opt out of addressing any topic, but the more evenings the Smithsons have these discussions, the less anyone opts out.

Your Family

• What are your family discussions at dinner like?

• *Wow, Pow, Holy Cow, How* might sound a bit corny to you or your kids, especially if they are teenagers. Another family tackles these topics by asking about "highs, lows, and how you saw God at work." Another family simply asks, "How's your heart?" More important than the labels you use are the conversations you have. Perhaps you could involve your kids in choosing the topics you'll discuss and the words you'll use to describe them.

> One night at dinner, I decided to talk with my three kids about unconditional love. I asked them, "Who in this family has recently expressed unconditional love to you?" All three answered in unison, "Our dog."
>
> —Ava

Sex Ed Talk ... or Talks

Dale and Nancy knew it was time to talk with their eleven-year-old about the birds and the bees. Ahead of time, they decided on the following principles.

- They wanted to have more than just "the talk" with Aaron. Instead they wanted to have a *series* of talks.

- Both parents wanted to be involved so that Aaron could ask either of them questions in the future.

- They wanted to give Aaron a book based on scriptural principles so he'd have a resource he could access later.

- In a year or two, they intended to invite Aaron to make a specific purity decision, but now their goal was to educate him and help him feel comfortable talking with them about his questions. So for these initial conversations, they wanted the environment to feel as normal as possible.

> *My wife and I have made our family motto "Tell me more." We use that phrase a lot in our conversations with our teenagers. We even made a small sign of those three words and hung it in our kitchen as a constant reminder of our family's commitment to conversation.*
>
> —Lucas

With these principles in mind, Nancy did some research online and selected a Bible-centered book geared for young teens. Once the book arrived, she and Dale showed it to Aaron, explaining that both parents would read the first chapter and underline the portions they especially wanted to talk over with him. Then they'd pass it to him to read. In a week or so, after they had all finished that chapter, the three of them would gather in Aaron's room at bedtime and discuss what they had underlined as well as any questions Aaron wanted to raise.

Week by week, chapter by chapter, they read through the book with Aaron. Even though Dale and Nancy don't know how much, if at all, Aaron consults the book now that they've finished studying it, they hope Aaron knows he can return not only to the book but also to both of his parents with his ongoing questions and dilemmas.

Your Family

- If you haven't already crossed this bridge in your family, what is your vision for your "birds and bees" talk with your child?

- If you have already had at least one talk with your child about sex, how did it go? What went well? What do you wish had been different?

- Regardless of your child's age and stage, what could you do to help your child turn to you in the future with their questions about sex?

 ## Current Event Springboards

"I'm pretty sure if I were alive when Jesus was, I would have hung out with Thomas," confessed Don, one of the parents we interviewed.

But Don's not afraid of his doubts, or his kids'. In fact, instead of hiding from tough questions, Don uses current events in the world to discuss questions with his kids, such as,

- Why would God allow that earthquake to kill so many people?

- Why isn't God empowering politicians to work together and fix what's broken in our country?

- Why doesn't God stop the religious wars that cause so many deaths and instead draw all people to worship Jesus Christ?

- Or just plain, What's wrong with America?

These questions are not easy, nor are Don's conversations with his kids. But Don is glad that his kids are learning not only that Don can handle their toughest questions but also that God can too.

Your Family

- When do you have your best opportunities to raise tough questions with your kids?

- How might current events function as a springboard that enables you to dive into deeper (and maybe even more difficult) conversations with your kids?

 ## Who Knows More Than You?

Matt and Amy have a good, honest relationship with their teenage daughter, but they know there are certain topics that Allie would rather discuss with someone other than them. Their concern was that Allie would turn to her peers for advice instead of consulting older, wiser adults.

So one Saturday afternoon they sat down together at their dining room table and shared a phrase with Allie that they had agreed on ahead of time: "Your friends don't know more than you." When Allie seemed to have grasped that principle, they spent some time brainstorming the names of other adults who, Allie recognized, knew more about life than either she or her friends. Working together, the three were able to identify aunts, teachers, friends of the family, and church members who had particular wisdom about topics like dating, stress, and parties. As Matt and Amy had hoped, Allie ended up with a list of adult mentors and sages so that when a future decision left her feeling lost and directionless, she would know where to turn.

> *Never stop talking with your kids. Never, ever stop.*
> —Colleen

Your Family

- What adults, if any, would your child go to for advice?

- If you're dissatisfied with this list, what ideas do you have for improving the quantity and/or quality of adults your child can talk to?

Sharing Your Testimony

One of the churches in our Sticky Faith Cohort program wanted to explore not only how many parents were talking with their kids about what God was showing them as parents in the here and now but also how many were telling their kids about their experiences with God in the past. The youth pastor at this church asked twenty high school students on a short-term mission trip if they knew how their parents decided to follow Christ.

Want to guess how many knew?

I'll give you a hint. The answer starts with the letter *Z*.

Zero. Zip. Zilch.

Another church in the Sticky Faith Cohort, upon hearing this, hosted a seminar for parents on how to share their testimony with their kids. Their two major problems were that they didn't carve out enough time for parents' questions and they didn't set up enough chairs for all who attended.

Although training for sharing your testimony is helpful, it is not essential. You might want to try following the pattern of Sue and Huan, who took their son out for dinner to share their stories of deciding to follow Jesus. They let him know what their lives had been like before they met Jesus, the experiences and people that drew them to Jesus, and the difference that Jesus has made since.

> We offer the Sticky Faith Cohort program, a yearlong coaching and training program for churches that want to dive more deeply into how our research can transform their entire congregation. For more information, visit *stickyfaith.org*.

Your Family

- If we asked your kids what led you to follow Jesus, what do you think they would say?
- What can you do to let your kids know more about the ways that following Jesus has changed you?

What if there are parts of my background that I wish my kids didn't know?

It's hard to answer that question without knowing more about you and your kids (not to mention your deepest, darkest sins), so please talk over that question with a close friend who knows your family well.

But we can say this: our observation is that parents are often overly cautious in sharing about their background, for fear of encouraging their kids to make those same unhealthy choices. The reality is that your kids have a host of other factors (friends, media, tempting situations) encouraging them to drink, do drugs, and have premarital sex, and these far outweigh whether Mom or Dad did so twenty-five years ago. In fact, knowing that you dealt with that same temptation may get your children to open up and talk with you more about it. If they are teenagers, chances are you're not going to share much that your kids haven't heard about before.

 ## What Would Happen Next?

Jamaal and Dee know that teenagers often make poor decisions when they haven't thought through the consequences of those choices ahead of time. So they came up with a family conversation game called What Would Happen Next?

Often while driving on long car trips, Jamaal or Dee give their teenagers a challenging ethical situation, such as, "You rode to a party with a friend who's started to drink. You're wondering if it's safe to ride home with her at the wheel. How would you handle that?"

One or both high school students describe what they think they would do. Then Jamaal or Dee asks, "Okay, if you did that, what would happen next?"

One of the kids then surmises what would be their next step, at which point Jamaal or Dee asks, "And then what would happen next?"

Thinking up scenarios that range from befriending an undocumented immigrant to counseling a friend with same-sex attraction,

We try to be intentional while resisting the temptation to turn everything into a teachable moment. When we were worried about our son being tempted to smoke pot because of some of the kids he was hanging out with at school, rather than lecture him or impose a whole bunch of rules, we talked with him about our honest fears as parents. Our son responded, "Mom and Dad, if I had wanted to smoke pot, I would have started four years ago. I'm scared to do it and I won't." When we heard that, we called off the dogs and realized we just need to keep talking with him.

—Macall

Jamaal and Dee are trying to prepare their kids for the tough ethical situations they may face. Their goal is to help their kids mentally journey through the twists and turns of teenage life ahead of time so that when they actually come to various forks in the road, they've thought about which lane to choose.

Your Family

- What do you think about Jamaal and Dee's premise that teenagers often make poor decisions because they haven't contemplated the consequences ahead of time?

- Given your child's age, what sorts of situations are most important to talk through with him or her?

 ## The (Aging) Kid Is the Expert

As his kids have gotten older, Terry has treated them as experts. In an effort to honor his college-age daughter's autonomy, he's tried to shift his tone from teaching her to testing ideas with her.

So his conversations with his daughter often start with phrases like,

> I've been wondering about this. What do you think?
> Try this on for size …
> Let me bounce this idea off you.
> I've been praying about this but still don't know what to do.
>   What advice do you have?

Terry finds that his daughter is often more likely to open up about some of her own uncertainties and struggles when he starts the conversation not just as a parent but also as a peer.

Your Family

- What do you think of Terry's theory that as his kids age, he should talk to them not just as a parent but also as a peer?

- If you think there's merit to this principle, what would it mean for your relationship with your oldest child?

 ## Late-Night Breath Check

When J.T. and Natalia's teenage children come home late at night from parties or a friend's house, the two of them are often asleep. When that happens, the kids know they need to wake up their mom (who is more of a night person) and give her a hug. Not only does that let her know they are safe; it also gives Natalia (who also has a keen sense of smell) a bit of a "sniff test." If her kids have been up to trouble, she can tell by the alcohol or smoke she smells.

Often after Natalia sits up in bed to give her kids a hug and tell them that she loves them, they quickly head back to their own bedroom to crash. But other nights, they want to debrief their evening with her. Some evenings they are downright chatty. As J.T. explains about his wife, "It is amazing what she can get out of them after midnight."

> I'm a single parent who only has my kids on the weekends, so I have to build in good conversation routines. After I pick them up, for the first forty-five minutes as we're driving back to my house, they aren't allowed to use any electronics. That has created a routine where we catch up without any distractions.
>
> —Patrice

Your Family

- How, if at all, do you connect with your teenage children when they get home late at night?

- What could you do, or ask your teenager to do, that would improve that connection?

Talk to Me or I'm Driving You to School

When Megan's son, Ryan, got his driver's license, Megan was excited that she would no longer need to drive him all around town. She figured this would add a handful of hours each week to her schedule.

But like many Sticky Faith parents, whether it was because Ryan was a captive audience or because he was often open to talking about what had just happened at school or tennis practice, Megan found that her best conversations with her son happened while they were in the car. While Megan was already envisioning what she could do with those free hours, she also grieved the loss of that precious time together.

So Megan told Ryan, "Many of our best talks happen in the car. Even though we won't be in the car as much, I'd like us to continue having those discussions. So if you don't talk to me around the house or at meals, then I'm going to have to go back to driving you to school and tennis every day."

Guess who all of a sudden got pretty chatty around the kitchen?

For a list of good questions to act as conversation starters, see *familyeducation.com*, especially "100 Questions to Ask Your Parents," *http://life.familyeducation.com/communication/family-time/36022.html*, and "100 Questions to Ask Your Kids," *http://life.familyeducation.com/communication/family-time/36021.html*.

Your Family

- This type of motivation (aka threat) might not work with your child. But as you think about what you will lose (or have lost) in car conversations as your teenager starts driving, what could help you continue to stay connected?

Our Family's Steps toward Sticky Faith

Take a few moments on your own, or with your spouse, your friends, or your small group, to reflect on some potential next steps toward Sticky Faith.

Sticky Findings

On a scale of 1 to 5 (with 1 being "we stink at this" and 5 being "we rock at this"), rate your family on the research findings presented in this chapter.

1| I both ask my kids questions about their faith and share about my own faith.

① ② ③ ④ ⑤

2| Our family is a safe place to talk about doubts and tough questions.

① ② ③ ④ ⑤

3| We discuss tricky and controversial subjects with our kids.

① ② ③ ④ ⑤

4| I use regular life events as conversation springboards with my kids.

① ② ③ ④ ⑤

5| I do not force my kids to agree with me; I let them arrive at their own conclusions.

① ② ③ ④ ⑤

6| While we realize that both parents need to be involved in faith dialogue, our kids have vibrant faith conversations with their mom (or stepmom or another female adult).

① ② ③ ④ ⑤

Sticky Ideas

1| When do you tend to have your best faith-related conversations with your children?

2| Given your ranking of the findings in the previous section, as well as the ideas you've read in this chapter, what one or two changes might you want to make in your family?

3| What can you do in the next few weeks or month to move toward these changes?

Chapter 9

Vacation!

Downtime Ways to Build Sticky Faith

I've lived with two different men for sixteen years each.

One is my husband. We have been married for sixteen years and are still going strong.

The other is my brother.

Matt is eighteen months younger than me, and we have always been close. We grew up sharing not only the same last name and parents but also the same sense of humor and commitment to our faith.

The week before Matt's wedding, I handwrote a four-page letter listing highlights of our relationship.

Like when we played hours of Go Fish at a picnic table and I kept winning. My secret? His mirrored sunglasses allowed me to see his cards.

Or the "rap" (quotation marks definitely warranted), which we adapted from a TV show, that repeated over and over again, "We have some fun but we get the job done." Even though we made up the song while we were in elementary school, almost every time we are together, we hum a few bars and chuckle.

Or sharing the back seat of the car, sometimes bickering with each other but more often playing games and serving as map readers (generally me) and sign readers (generally Matt) to help our mom as she was driving.

All three of these memories happened on family vacations. In fact, about 50 percent of the memories I included in Matt's prewedding letter were from trips together.

Matt and I went to the same schools, were on the same swim team, were part of the same church, and had adjoining bedrooms fifty weeks per year. But half of my fondest memories are from the two weeks each year when we were on a family vacation.

Sticky Findings

1 ## The Priority of Time Away Together

By far, the most common theme in Sticky Faith parents' descriptions of their vacations is that they simply did them. They made them a priority. Despite all that parents were juggling, they didn't drop that ball.

In the midst of this nearly universal priority placed on family travel, there was great variety in what these trips were like. Some families drove to the next state; others flew to the next continent.

Some loved camping and sleeping under the stars; others loved resorts and sleeping under a down comforter.

Some enjoyed returning to the same location annually; others determined to head to a new destination every year.

Some wanted as much adventure and excitement as possible; others preferred decompressing by the pool, doing as little as possible.

Regardless of the size of the vacation budget, these Sticky Faith families invested multiple days each year to be together, away from the normal hassles and pressures felt by adults and kids alike. As one dad described, "Whether we stay close or go far, our trips together build trust. This might sound strange, but it is almost like we buy back family intimacy on every vacation. The bonding that happens is worth every penny."

2 ## Kids Have a Voice

While this next finding is not as pervasive as the previous one, Sticky Faith parents tended to give their kids a voice (and even a vote) at various points along the vacation process. Some parents involved their kids *before* the holiday in helping select the destination. One dad said, "I stopped going on vacation with my parents when I was sixteen, because they kept visiting historical sites that I found boring. We've let our son help choose our destinations so he will look forward to the trips."

Other parents involved their kids *during* their travels by letting them decide together what the family did each afternoon. A few

---

What if my kids say they don't want to go on a family vacation?

My brother and I should have been excited, but in reality we dreaded an upcoming ten-day trip to Europe.

Why? Because we knew we would miss our friends.

Why would we miss our friends? Because we were fifteen and seventeen, and that's how teenagers feel.

If your teenagers don't want to go on vacation, odds are good they are worried about what they will miss back home. It doesn't make sense to us adults, but for a teenager, a week in paradise with family is no substitute for missing a three-hour party where "all their friends" will be.

When our travel schedule means our kids miss something important, I often ask this question: What can I do to make this up to you? I don't want to ask that question too often, lest we create a perennial parent-child bartering system. But when it's something out of our kids' control (such as a previously scheduled family event) that means they have to miss something important to them, I want them to know I care about what they care about.

I never want to buy them something to compensate. I figure that since they are disappointed about missing something social, that should be offset by another social activity, such as having an overnighter at our house or going to a movie with some friends.

If they don't want to go on vacation for another reason—like they think they won't have fun with just their family—then try asking a similar question: What can we do on vacation that would be fun? In the long run, your child's knowing that you care and want to listen to their ideas and are willing to nuance your vacation accordingly is far more important than whether you squeeze in that final museum together.

---

parents even gave each family member a turn in selecting what the family did that day. One mom we interviewed explained, "We ask each family member ahead of time, 'What's the one thing you want to do or the one place you want to go during this vacation?' It makes it a lot easier for our kids to spend an afternoon doing something they don't really want to do, when they know that in the next few days they will get to choose the family outing."

Still other parents engaged their kids *after* each day's events by inviting them to write down highlights in a family scrapbook or in individual journals. If that felt forced, some families jettisoned the journals and circled their kids for conversation around the campfire or dinner table instead.

Sticky Ideas

 ## The Best Ice Cream We Can Find

Roger's work schedule often means he doesn't make it home for dinner. So for Roger and his family, vacations are an opportunity to reclaim meals together, especially dinner. Not because their dinners are fancy or expensive but because Roger's family takes their time and views dinner as more of a process than a meal. If they are at restaurants, they slowly peruse the menu, experiment with appetizers, main dishes, and desserts they've never tried before, and try to savor every bite.

> Every time we take a trip, our two daughters fight like cats and dogs the first two days. But as our vacation adventures unfold, they bond together. Our times away bring our girls together.
> —Alisha

If they are staying in an apartment or a condominium and are cooking for themselves, each morning they choose the dinner menu for that night. In the midst of their other activities that day, Roger and his family purchase as many ingredients as possible from a local food market so that their dish is both fresh and native. Every evening, not only does the family eat together; they usually also prepare the meal and clean the kitchen together.

In addition, Roger's family makes it a quest to find the best ice cream in each city they visit. It takes some dedication, and often a scoop both after lunch and after dinner. (Yes, it's a sacrifice!) But by the end of each vacation, they have determined the winning ice cream shop and reward that shop with quite a bit of business.

Your Family

- What role do meals play in your vacations?
- Perhaps you don't want to be as focused on food as Roger's family is, but are there ways that food (especially dinners) could become a passport to greater memories during your travels?

Scripture in the Sierras

As with the families of many Sticky Faith parents we interviewed, camping was a ritual for Christopher and his two daughters. Being a single parent who longs for deeper relationships with his fifth- and seventh-graders, Christopher loves their days of hiking, fishing, and exploring.

One of their rituals is to bring board games and a Bible on a mountain climb. Once they arrive at the peak, they play games, squeezing in a few paragraphs of Scripture here and there.

Sometimes the Bible passages don't yield much conversation, or what they read feels abstract and a bit confusing, especially to the fifth-grader. But other times what they read is right on target. God's Word perfectly captures what they are feeling and experiencing as they are surrounded by the wonder of God's creation.

Your Family

- How, if at all, is God's Word part of your family vacations?
- What baby steps could you take to include some Scripture in your travels?

Family History Trips

Having grown up in Puerto Rico, Javier decided to take his wife, Lynda, and his kids back to his hometown to meet some of his friends. That first geographical foray into Javier's history went so well that Javier and Lynda decided to take their kids to visit other locations that had been important in their past.

Like their first apartment in Chicago.

And their first home, which happened to be in London.

And their next home, which was in Cleveland (just a tad less glamorous than London).

As they visited the cities of their past, they introduced their kids to their favorite restaurants and haunts as well as to the people who shaped them into who they are today.

Your Family

- Can you imagine taking your kids to visit one of the cities where you lived in the past, either before or after you got married?

- What would you hope visiting that town or city would accomplish for your family?

 ## Cultural Conversations

A major goal in Mary Sue and Steve's family vacations is to expose their kids to various cultures. At times that means traveling out of the country. But more often it means visiting a nearby state. Or even driving only a few hours from home to transplant themselves into urban or rural contexts that seem vastly different from their suburban norm.

Mary Sue and Steve make it a point to ask their kids questions about the culture they are visiting, such as,

- What do you notice here that's the same as where we live?
- What's different?
- What do you like about this culture?
- What about this culture feels different or challenging for you?
- What signs of wealth do you see in this culture?

- What signs of poverty do you observe?
- How do families tend to interact in this culture?
- How do people seem to live out their faith in this culture?

As our world flattens, Mary Sue and Steve want to give their kids the skills they need to float from culture to culture.

Your Family

- What types of cultures are your kids exposed to on your vacations?
- How would talking openly about those cultures expand your relationships as well as their view of the world?

 ## Day Trippin'

Since her divorce, Fiona treasures her alternating Saturdays with her daughters. After swinging by the farmer's market for some fresh fruit and vegetables, she and the girls look at each other and ask, "Where are we going to go today?"

For Fiona's family, Saturdays are minivacations, chances to drive an hour or two and see a different part of the Northern California region they call home. To make it more interesting, the mom and daughters take turns choosing their journey's end point. The older daughter often selects the beach at the Santa Cruz boardwalk. Her sister tends to opt for the hustle and bustle of San Francisco. Fiona usually targets parks and forests that are within driving distance.

Fiona keeps a notepad to track where the threesome has been. The notepad has two purposes: it helps capture family memories, and it reminds them of whose turn it is to choose the destination.

Your Family

- What role do weekends, or even just Saturdays, play in your family's vacation habits?
- When in the near future can your family get away for a day? How can you involve your kids in creating your itinerary?

School-Inspired Sites

Ron and Marguerite were so proud of all that their two teenagers, Ben and Amy, were learning at school. In order to cement both the knowledge they had acquired as well as their family relationships, Ron and Marguerite decided that when possible, they would factor Ben and Amy's academic subjects into their touring plans. Traveling outside of the US wasn't an option financially, but that was just fine. There were plenty of pilgrimages they could take within America's borders.

Studying the Civil War yielded a winter break trip through the Southeast.

The science unit on space exploration was a perfect jumping-off point for an April trip to Florida that included not just Disney World but also NASA's Kennedy Space Center.

The book report on *The Scarlet Letter* evolved into a summer vacation through New England.

Marguerite finds that her kids are more excited about their trips because they know that they will get to see in person some of the sites they have been reading about at school.

We took our kids to Colorado to climb one of its fourteen-thousand-foot peaks. Our two teenagers made it to the top first. I made it next. My husband, who had just finished a crazy season at work and hadn't had the chance to train at all, was struggling to finish. So our oldest son headed back down and helped my husband with his pack so he could make it up. My husband has been the boys' coach and always helped them out. Now the boys are bigger than he is, and the roles are reversed. When my husband made it to the top, he said, "The next time we climb, I'm training."

—Catherine

Your Family

- Maybe a trip to see the sites connected with your kids' studies isn't viable financially. How could you link what your kids have learned recently to your next trip, wherever your destination?

Local Hotel Staycation

Melissa and Todd have realized that what their kids like the most about vacations is staying in a hotel. For eight- and ten-year-olds, it doesn't really matter where the hotel is as long as it has a swimming pool and a continental breakfast bursting with the sugared cereals that Mom and Dad forbid at home.

So every once in a while, instead of driving for a few days or flying for a few hours, the four of them head to a nearby hotel and enjoy local sites and restaurants. With minimal travel time and few travel headaches, they end up with more time together just to relax.

Your Family

- What might your family lose by taking a staycation instead of a trip out of town?
- What might your family gain?

 ## Fruit of the Spirit

Even though Vera and James knew it might be a stretch, they thought their three kids were ready for a weekend backpacking trip. As a family that likes to hike, they had spent several Saturday afternoons tromping through their local mountains, so backpacking seemed like a logical next step (or more accurately, fifteen thousand steps).

But just in case, Vera and James invited another family to go with them. They figured that having buddies along would improve their kids' attitude and that having another family watching would encourage Vera and James to be more patient with their own kids. (Besides, they had a lot of trail mix to carry, so a few other adults to share the load seemed like a plus.)

Since the kids from both families had been learning a song about the fruit of the Spirit at church, the four parents figured that would make a great theme for their weekend. As they set off on the trail, the parents told the kids to look for signs of group members showing the fruit of the Spirit, such as patience with a sibling who needs help crossing a stream or self-control displayed by an adult who waits last for s'mores after dinner.

At the end of each day, around a campfire, the kids taught the parents the fruit of the Spirit song from church. Then everyone took turns sharing how they had seen those qualities in each other that day. This evening ritual was a great way to recap the day as well as affirm the godly character of both generations.

Your Family

- What sorts of theme verses might fit your next family vacation?
- How would talking over how you've seen those verses in action each day change your conversations at dinner or later in the evening?

 ## Vacation Sketches

Part of what Paul loves most about vacations is that they are his best chance to experiment with art. During the rest of the year, his family/work/church merry-go-round leaves him little to no time to sketch or paint. His annual family vacation is his primary opportunity to step off his crazy carousel and sit quietly for an hour with his watercolors and sketchpad.

Paul finds it especially relaxing to paint scenes from the vacation he is on, whether it's the view from their hotel or a scene of his three kids swimming in the lake they visited yesterday. Looking over his shoulder, Paul's wife, Corrina, has been struck regularly by Paul's ability to capture not just what their family has seen but also how they have felt when they are together out of town.

Instead of leaving these pictures in the portfolio Paul kept under his bed, Corrina decided to display them. She bought a handful of inexpensive frames so she could mount one painting from each trip in the hallway leading to their kids' bedrooms. Now, in addition to the vacation mementos they have sprinkled around their living room and family room, they have a personal and permanent art exhibit depicting their holiday highlights.

Your Family

- What vacation mementos do you have in your home? What memories or feelings do they evoke in you and your kids?
- How could you make those keepsakes (or ones you will collect in the future) a more central part of your home decor?

 ## Church Destinations

While some families think of vacations as a time to skip church, Thomas and Jane view them as a time to celebrate and explore different churches. On their trips, Thomas and Jane have taken their children to visit and worship at a number of churches with historical significance, such as Christ Church in Philadelphia (the home church of fifteen signers of the Declaration of Independence) and New York Avenue Presbyterian Church in Washington, D.C. (Abraham Lincoln's congregation).

When they are not visiting well-known churches, Thomas and Jane use weekends away with their kids to expose their teenage children to churches that are of a different denomination or have a worship style different from their home church. By exposing their kids to churches of all flavors, they are expanding their children's view of what it looks like to worship and serve God.

Your Family

- What role have churches played in your vacations up to now?
- If you're not satisfied with your answer, what changes would you like to make the next time your family travels?

Our Family's Steps toward Sticky Faith

Take a few moments on your own, or with your spouse, your friends, or your small group, to reflect on some potential next steps toward Sticky Faith.

Sticky Findings

On a scale of 1 to 5 (with 1 being "we stink at this" and 5 being "we rock at this"), rate your family on the research findings presented in this chapter.

1| Our family makes vacations a priority in our schedule.

① ② ③ ④ ⑤

2| Our kids have a voice in what we do during our vacations.

① ② ③ ④ ⑤

Sticky Ideas

1| What about your vacations seems to make the most difference in your family's relationships or faith?

2| Given your ranking of the findings in the previous section, as well as the ideas you've read in this chapter, what one or two changes might you want to make in your family?

3| What can you do in the next few weeks or month to move toward these changes?

Chapter 10

Home Sticky Home

Making Your House a Hub of Faith

Home base.

Whether it's capture the flag, hide-and-seek, or just regular ol' tag, every kid knows that when they are being chased or simply need a break from danger, they head to home base. If they are touching the tree or standing on the towel that represents home base, no one can attack them. It's their chance to shout encouraging or strategic advice to their teammates. It's their opportunity to catch their breath for a few moments before diving back into the game.

For kids, home base represents safety.

Can the same be said of your home?

When your kids long for some encouragement, do they head home?

When your kids need to feel protected, do they veer toward your driveway?

In most families, as kids get older, they want to be home less and less. Six-year-olds tell their parents, "I want to go home." Sixteen-year-olds rarely do.

It's normal and healthy for maturing young people to spend less time at home and more time with their friends. The life of a teenager doesn't orbit around their parents; they feel a strong attraction toward school, sports, clubs, work, and friends.

While the parents we interviewed had busy kids, their homes were still magnetic enough that their kids wanted to do more than just grab food and sleep there. These young people were drawn to their homes not necessarily because they were large.

Or clean.

Or fancy.

It was because their homes had maintained the same sense of safety that home base offered in freeze tag. In the midst of all the forces pulling parents and kids away from each other, the home kept exerting a gravitational pull that often brought family members closer to each other and to God.

Sticky Findings

1 ### It's Important to Make Your Home a Place Where Your Kids' Friends Feel Welcome

By far, the most dominant theme in our discussions with fifty amazing parents about their homes is that they wanted their homes to be places where both their kids and their kids' friends felt accepted. Whether home was a small urban condominium, a two-story house on a suburban cul-de-sac, or a large property complete with a swimming pool and fire pit, parents tried to create an environment in which children and teenagers felt welcome.

A few parents mentioned that having their kids' friends over gave them a window into youth culture—and even their own kids' lives—that they wouldn't have otherwise. As one mom with college students recalled, "Especially in middle school and high school, my best tool for understanding my kids was hearing them talk to their friends in our car or at our house. We did anything we could to engage their world—to listen and to watch. My husband and I began to understand which questions we could ask and which were embarrassing."

We want our kids to understand that life done well is done in community.
—Kenton

2 The Power of Creating Boundaries around Technology

But creating a welcoming space for kids doesn't mean granting kids permission to do whatever they want, whenever they want to. A second dominant theme in our fifty parents' descriptions of their homes is that they limit their kids' use of technology.

These boundaries are needed because of the way young people today are marinated in media. Let's consider together a generation whose lives are heavily flavored by technology.

- Fifty-eight percent of this generation possess a desktop computer.
- Sixty-one percent own a laptop.
- Eighteen percent use a tablet or e-reader.

But the real king of all technology is the device in their pocket. Almost 90 percent of this generation carry a cell phone.[1]

When asked to describe their cell phone in one word, this generation answered, "Awesome," "Great," "Good," "Love," "Excellent," "Useful," and "Convenient."[2]

You might be thinking that some of those words don't sound very adolescent. Especially the words *useful* and *convenient*. That's because the generation I'm describing isn't teenagers. It's adults.

Are young people avid users of technology? You bet. But the data suggests that while teenagers may be digital natives, we adults are fast-adapting digital immigrants. Before we judge teenagers for their quick-texting thumbs and seemingly permanent earbuds, we adults need to put down our smartphones and think about our own media consumption.

Eighty-three percent of young people are involved in social networking. So are 77 percent of their parents.[3]

Among all US household types, the traditional nuclear family with two parents and children under eighteen is more likely than other household types — such as single adults or couples without children — to have cell phones and use the internet.[4]

Often parents use this technology to improve their relationships with their kids. After all, texting can help parents stay in touch with their children throughout the day. Social media allows parents to take the pulse of their kids' lifestyle choices and friendships.[5]

But the parents we interviewed have recognized that the same technology that builds bridges can also build walls. Kids are so focused on sharing videos online with friends five miles away that they become numb to family members sitting five feet from them. Parents become immersed in their computers, barely noticing when their kids enter and leave the family room. Given how technology cuts across generations, many wise parents impose limits not only on their kids but also on themselves.

3 Family Dinners — Magical or Mythical?

Blog posts and books tout the benefits of family dinners. Are regular family dinners part of a magical formula that can bring harmony and happiness to your home?

The best answer from research is, Sort of.

We always made sure that no matter where we've lived, we've had a big enough table for all of us to gather around and eat. The table is the place where lots of important conversations happen, not just around dinner but at breakfast or lunch or throughout the day.

—Leticia

Kids who have dinner with their families seem to make better choices and avoid disorders and high-risk behaviors including depression, delinquency, and drug and alcohol use. But when researchers took into account other differences between families who have dinner together and those who don't (such as differences in overall relationship quality, parental monitoring, and shared activities), the effects of family dinners diminished drastically.

In other words, the parents who value family dinners seem also to build healthy and caring bonds with their kids in a host of other ways.[6]

Family dinner conversations are a bright light in these parents' relationships with their children, but they are only one star in a constellation of connections that already shines brightly. So while dinner is a natural opportunity for families to communicate, it's not the secret sauce of Sticky Faith families. The ongoing involvement and conversation between parents and kids is what matters most, whether or not it happens over a tablecloth.

I wish we had eaten meals every night together when our kids were younger. Now that our kids are teenagers, they are all going different directions in the evening. I wish we had taken advantage of those early years when our kids weren't as busy.

—Spencer

Sticky Ideas

Actually Being Home

Parents committed to building enduring faith through their homes often start with a simple, basic step. They regularly choose to be at home with their kids.

For parents to slash activities from their own schedules is certainly a challenge. But many families find that the need to trim activities from their kids' schedules is an even larger barrier to time at home together.

Many families create policies that state how many sports and clubs their kids can participate in at any one time. (Generally it was one or two.) To avoid year-round busyness, others designate certain seasons, such as summer or winter, as sports-free months in their homes. As one mom described, "Six or seven years ago we eliminated most activities for the kids during the winter. From November to March is our time to be home, eat meals together, and do fun things at night and on weekends. That was probably the smartest choice we ever made as parents. The rest of the year, our family feels somewhat divided and fractured by multiple kids and multiple activities, but winter is our time to enjoy being together."

Your Family

- How does your family schedule help or hinder the relational quality of your home life?

- What might you be able to trim from your schedule or your kids' schedules to help your family be home together more?

 ## Facebook Friends

At the time that we interviewed parents, Facebook was the leading social media site among teenagers. Parents commonly mentioned that their kids are allowed to have a Facebook account only if the parents are allowed to be their kids' "friends" and are thus granted access to their kids' posts. Some parents require password access to all social media accounts so their kids know that their online lives can't be hidden from Mom and Dad's occasional check-ins.

Many parents promise their kids that they won't post directly on their kids' pages. (There are few embarrassments greater than Mom chiming in about your friends' clothing choices.) Parents want to read, not comment. If their kids are posting publicly, they believe that responsible parenting includes scanning their comments, pictures, and "likes" as yet one more way of staying informed.

Your Family

- What rules do you have for your kids' use of social media?

- How would monitoring your kids' posts affect your parenting and your relationship with your child?

 ## Cell Phone Contract

Dan and Denise's fourteen-year-old son has two cell phone contracts: one with his cell phone carrier and one with them. In order to clarify their family's cell phone expectations and protocol, Dan and Denise printed the following guidelines and had their son sign them and post them in his room.

1. It is our phone. We bought it. We pay for it. We are loaning it to you. Aren't we great?

2. We will always know the password.

3. If it rings, answer it. Say hello and use good manners. Never ignore a phone call if the screen reads "Mom" or "Dad."

4. Hand the phone to one of your parents before bed every night.

5. If it falls into the toilet, smashes on the ground, or vanishes into thin air, you are responsible for the replacement costs or repairs.

6. Put it away in public (for example, in church, in restaurants, in movie theaters, wherever you are with other people). You are not rude; do not allow your phone to change that.

7. Do not use your phone to lie to, fool, or deceive another human being. Do not involve yourself in conversations that are hurtful to others. Be a good friend first.

We've helped our family relationships by not allowing computers or TVs in our kids' rooms. Wherever the TV or computer is, our kids will be. So if it's not in their bedrooms, our family interacts with each other more.

—Travis

8. Do not text, email, or say anything through this device you would not say in person.

9. No porn. Nothing you wouldn't want your mother to see.

10. Do not send or receive pictures of your private parts or anyone else's private parts. Don't laugh. Despite your intelligence, someday you might be tempted to do this. It is risky and could ruin your life.

11. Take pictures, but don't forget to live your experiences. Keep your eyes up. See the world happening around you. Stare out a window. Listen to the birds. Take a walk.

12. Leave your phone home sometimes and be okay with that decision. Learn to live without it.

13. Download music that is new or classic or different from what your peers listen to. Your generation has access to

music like never before in history. Take advantage of that gift. Expand your horizons.

14. Play a game with words or puzzles or brainteasers every now and then.

15. You will mess up. We will take away your phone. We will sit down and talk about it. We will start over again. We will always be learning. We are on your team. We are in this together.

Your Family

- What clear rules do you have for cell phone usage in your family?
- After reading this list of guidelines, are there any rules you'd like to add?

 ## *The Phone Basket*

"Can you please put your phone away so I can talk to you?"

That was a request that Jay and Stacey commonly had to make of their two teenage daughters. Truth be told, Jay and Stacey's daughters weren't the only ones who spent more time staring at a screen than engaging with other family members. As parents juggling multiple work, church, and family responsibilities, Jay and Stacey would often let their own "quick checks" of their phones after dinner expand into an evening focused more on communicating with friends across the country than on talking with family across the dining room table.

> *Our home is a refuge to us and to others. We open our doors to family, friends, and our church's youth group. We want our house to be the place.*
>
> —Rolf

So Jay and Stacey created one simple rule in their home: when you walk into the house, you put your phone in a basket in the living room. This is true not just for the four who live there but also for friends who visit.

Initially the phone basket prompted a fair amount of complaining and eye rolling from their teenagers. But the girls and their friends have ended up liking it. Instead of sitting shoulder-to-shoulder in the same room staring at their phones, they all look each other in the eye now and talk to each other.

While not directly related to Sticky Faith at home, here's an interesting cell phone corollary: If you or other family members or friends are tempted to check phones while out at a restaurant, you might want to follow my brother's policy. When he goes out to eat with friends, they all put their cell phones in a stack on the table. If anyone reaches for their phone before the bill comes, that person has to cover the entire group's bill.

Your Family

- How, if at all, do cell phones affect your family's face-to-face communication?

- If you don't like your answer to the previous question, what boundaries might you want to put into place to improve your family relationships?

Stocking the Fridge

In describing the glue that makes their homes a social hub for their kids and their kids' friends, multiple families pointed to the power of food. As one dad summarized, "If we stock our fridge and cupboard, kids come over a lot. It gets pricey, but it's worth it."

Some parents involve their kids in planning the food they want to have for guests. That way the kids learn more about hospitality and food budgeting, while choosing snacks that reflect the vibe they want to create for their friends.

Your Family

- What role, if any, do snacks play in how your kids and your kids' friends feel about spending time at your house?

- How can you involve your kids in budgeting for and choosing the food they want to offer to their friends?

Homework Room

For many families, homework time means that everyone heads to their room and ignores everybody else. Shami wanted something different for her family. She had a vision of homework time being something that brought family members together instead of sending them to separate corners of the house.

So she turned her home office into a homework room. She

What if my child doesn't want to keep their room clean?

In the midst of our discussions with Sticky Faith parents about their kids' bedrooms, two facts became clear. First, the state of kids' bedrooms is a main source of conflict and stress in a family's home. Second, amazing parents who show great unanimity in the majority of parenting practices show great disagreement in their views about how to respond to their kids' cluttered rooms.

Some believe that raising responsible kids means teaching them how to steward their own belongings and space. Beds need to be made, desk surfaces need to be clean, and clothes need to be put away.

Other parents feel that in the midst of all the potential conflict they could have with their kids, clean rooms just aren't all that important. Kids need to do regular chores to help keep the common areas of the house clean, but their room is their own space. Other than a monthly thorough Saturday cleaning, they can keep it as they want.

Since there was no trend in parents' policies about clean bedrooms, it's challenging for us to make specific recommendations to you. But we can invite you to reflect on the following questions.

- How can you make sure that you and your spouse are sending consistent messages to your kids about their rooms?

- How do your background and your own issues (for example, your discomfort with clutter, your tendency toward hoarding) taint how you interact with your kids about their rooms?

- If messy or dirty bedrooms are causing conflict in your home, is it worth the fight to have the kids clean them? Why or why not?

still has a desk there, but by clustering two additional desks on one side of the room, Shami has given her daughter and her husband their own workspace also. Now when her daughter is studying and Shami and her husband are at their computers, the three of them are all in the same room working together.

Your Family

- How do your kids' homework habits affect your family communication and time together?
- What creative use of your house could make homework a time that unites you instead of separates you?

Faith in Every Room

As followers of Jesus, Gloria and Edgar felt that their house should reflect their faith. More specific, their goal was that in every room there would be at least a memento or book that reminded their family, as well as others visiting, of their commitment to Christ.

So near the doorway in their living room they placed a small painting that spoke of the beauty of God's creation. Next to the stove in their kitchen was a rock with a cross carved on it. Each of their kids got to choose one item for their bedroom that reflected their faith, whether it was a single book or a large inspirational poster. Without being overwhelming or imposing, Christ-centered art and messages that Edgar and Gloria have placed in their home are an external expression of their internal faith.

Your Family

- What signs of your faith are already visible in your house?
- Are there any changes you'd like to make in your home decor to more clearly reflect your commitment to Jesus?

The Praying Chair

Tired of the blank looks they received when they asked their kids, "Who wants to pray for dinner?" Rodney and Jackie designated a "praying chair" at their kitchen table. Whoever sits at that chair gets to pray for the meal.

Sometimes when the kids set the table, one of them will put themselves in the praying chair. If the parents set the table, they usually reserve the chair for one of the kids who hasn't prayed in a while. Rodney and Jackie's hope is that by taking turns praying for the meal, their kids will feel more comfortable praying aloud, whether or not food is involved.

Your Family

• What rituals do you follow in praying for your meals?

• How are your kids involved in those rituals?

• What are your kids learning about prayer from the way you or they pray for meals?

The Special Plates

When Sal and Karen's two daughters were in elementary school, each girl had a school assignment requiring them to color on a white ceramic plate and then heat the plate in a pottery kiln to make their art masterpiece permanent. Over the years, the girls have given Sal and Karen similar plates for Father's Day and Mother's Day to commemorate how much they appreciate them as parents.

Since all four family members now have their own special plates, Sal and Karen decided to put them to good use. Every night at dinner, one family member gets to eat off their special plate. If it's April's turn to use her special plate, April gets to say the blessing for the meal, and then sometime during dinner, each member of the family shares something special they see in April. April's sister, Leah, might comment that she appreciates that April likes to spend time with her or lets her borrow her clothes. Sal and Karen might recollect a positive character quality they have seen April demonstrate, like how she was compassionate to the girl who was being bullied at school or how she worked very hard on her science project. Sal likes to affirm the way his daughters are good sisters to each other, so he might comment on the way April cheered up Leah after a disappointing swim meet or test score. If a guest is staying for dinner, often the guest will receive a special plate, which has prompted some great conversation and encouragement.

Sal is quick to confess that their family is far from perfect at this practice. He admits, "Some nights the girls have just been bickering with each other and then have to say something kind about each other. While that's a bit awkward, overall the special plates have helped create a positive and uplifting tone at our meals. Our girls, now fourteen and seventeen, are the best of friends, something their school friends find astounding."

Your Family

- How affirming are your dinner conversations?
- Whether it's a special plate every night or a special cup once a week, what could you do to help your family regularly practice affirming each other?

 ## Conversation Couch

Joyce felt that instead of being a hub of refuge and relationship, her house was more of a pit stop for her teenagers to grab a few meals and a few hours of sleep. As an interior designer, she is aware of the messages that a space communicates, and she decided to designate a special place in her house for family conversation.

She and her husband declared a couch in the living room, which was removed from the foot traffic between the kitchen and the bedrooms, as their "conversation couch." Joyce explained to her kids that if they ever wanted a more focused chat with either parent, they could ask them to come to that couch. And if the parents wanted that kind of talk with their kids, they could invite them there as well. Of course, conversations could happen anywhere in the house. And the couch is used every day for purposes other than deep conversation. But Joyce has found that having a few feet of cushions appointed for conversation is a catalyst for family discussions that might not happen otherwise.

Your Family

- Where do conversations tend to happen in your house?
- How, if at all, would designating a special place for family discussions enhance your relationships?

Bible Wall

When Keyanna and Delonte have felt like they were drowning in life's challenges, Scripture has often been their lifesaver. Because of the way they treasure God's Word, Keyanna and Delonte have created a Bible wall in their kitchen to help their elementary-age sons appreciate particular passages. Every week, they post the Scripture memory verse from their church's children's ministry on that wall to help all four family members memorize it. If one of their boys is facing a certain struggle, Keyanna or Delonte will share a relevant passage with him and hang it on the wall. The Bible wall not only gives the family hope for how God will help them in the future; it reminds them of the way God has fulfilled his promises for them already.

I never read the Bible as much as I wish I had with my kids. We talk about it every once in a while, but I wish it was more a part of our daily lives.

—Rick

Your Family

- What role does Scripture memorization play in your family's faith journey?
- How could a wall, corner, or bulletin board in your home become a tool that stimulates your family's appreciation for God's Word?

Christmas Card Dinner Prayers

Beth wanted her kids to experience the joy of praying for others' needs. Yet if Beth were honest, it was hard enough for her to keep track of her own friends' needs, let alone try to involve her three kids in praying for others, especially on a regular basis.

Beth knew she needed a system that is fun, easy, and in sync with the rhythms of their home. So last January, she stacked the Christmas cards her family had received the month prior in a basket next to the kitchen table. Every night before dinner, one of her kids reaches in the basket and chooses a card. In addition to blessing the food, her family also prays for the person or family who sent them the Christmas card.

Through one basket and a bit of forethought, Beth has found a great way to bring the power of Christmas and prayer to her dinner table throughout the year.

Your Family

- What rhythms does your family have to help you pray for others outside of your family?
- Like Beth, what system could you use (perhaps one that involves visual prompts and is tied to a regular meal or bedtime routine) to help your family remember to pray for friends, other families, and ministries?

 ## Seeing the World — Literally

Ramon and Elisabeth wanted to help their three elementary-age children realize that the world is much bigger than their little corner of it. So they have hung a large world map on the wall parallel to their dining room table. When world events come up in family conversations, Ramon and Elisabeth can show their kids where those events occurred. When guests mention a place they've visited or a place where they've served on a mission trip, Ramon and Elisabeth can point to those locations on the map. While their kids haven't yet traveled outside of the US, they have talked about, visualized, and prayed for nations on every continent.

Your Family

- In what ways do the items in your home help expand your kids' view of the world and God's work in it?

- As you think about where you spend the most time in your home with your kids (likely your kitchen, family room, or dining room), what visual cues could help stretch your family's faith and prayer life?

Our Family's Steps toward Sticky Faith

Take a few moments on your own, or with your spouse, your friends, or your small group, to reflect on some potential next steps toward Sticky Faith.

Sticky Findings

On a scale of 1 to 5 (with 1 being "we stink at this" and 5 being "we rock at this"), rate your family on the research findings presented in this chapter.

1| Our home is a place where our kids and their friends feel welcome.

① ② ③ ④ ⑤

2| I limit my kids' use of technology at home.

① ② ③ ④ ⑤

3| I limit my own use of technology at home.

① ② ③ ④ ⑤

4| We have quality family conversations in our home, whether at dinner or at other times.

① ② ③ ④ ⑤

Sticky Ideas

1 | In what ways does your home strengthen your kids' relationships with you and with God?

2 | Given your ranking of the findings in the previous section, as well as the ideas you've read in this chapter, what one or two changes might you want to make in your family?

3 | What can you do in the next few weeks or month to move toward these changes?

Chapter 11

Service That Sticks

Putting Family Faith to Work

"My son has more opportunities to serve through Boy Scouts than he does at our church."

"My daughter has learned more about building relationships with homeless people through her school's required community service than she has through our high school ministry."

As our team has shared about Sticky Faith, we have heard these statements repeatedly from parents across the nation. Whether it's through Scouts or a service club at school, kids often have their most meaningful and, dare we say, Sticky service experiences outside of the church.

On the one hand, it's good for students to grasp that God's love and grace flow through all sorts of channels.

On the other hand, I believe that the best hope for our world is the church. I yearn for the day when we as the church are known for what we are *for* instead of what we are *against*. I pray that the long list of "what the church is for" includes remarkable Christ-centered care for the least, the last, and the lost.

Of all this guide's chapters, this one is the hardest for our family to live out. Our church has many, many strengths, but engaging families in service locally or globally isn't one of them.

So together with our kids, Dave and I have picked some low-hanging fruit from the family service tree. Most summers, our kids do a special fundraiser for a ministry we choose. (One year our kids raised $733 selling brownies and Rice Krispies treats to friends; that's a lot of sugar exported from our kitchen.) We sponsor a child in India through a monthly donation. Every once in a while we take our kids shopping so they can use their own money to fill a Christmas shoebox or participate in a food drive. But in the fabric of our family's life, those events feel more like nubs of yarn than like threads that weave their way through our priorities. Unlike every other area of our research, when I speak at conferences and churches about our Sticky service findings, I usually talk about other families instead of my own.

You might think that makes me a hypocrite.

You are probably right. There is a degree of hypocrisy in urging families to hop on the service highway when my own family is only about two-thirds down the on-ramp.

But hopefully my disclosure of our family's slow headway will lift any self-condemnation you may be feeling as you've worked through this guide. As we said in chapter 1, we are all in process. If Sticky Faith is a marathon, there will be some laps that you'll feel you're making good time. But there will be others where you'll feel you're frozen at the starting line. Or even worse, your calf is cramping and you're not even sure you have the strength to don your running shoes and head for the course.

The good news is that your family isn't running the faith race alone. Whether you're hitting the wall or you've gotten a second wind, you can draft off others who are a few steps ahead of you.

In no other area of our research is this truer for me personally. I'm drafting off a good friend whose desk at Fuller Seminary is about seven feet from mine. Our associate director at the Fuller Youth Institute, Brad Griffin, and his wife, Missy, help set the pace for our family when it comes to engaging in Sticky service.

When Brad and Missy's oldest daughter, Anna, was four years old, their church sponsored a Christmas box outreach to impoverished children in Ensenada. Long after they turned in the box full of toys and toothbrushes, Anna kept reminding Brad and Missy to pray for their recipient, Ariana—both that the gifts would make a difference and that God would remember her (just in case he needed reminding).

But Anna wasn't satisfied with praying for Ariana. Anna wanted to meet her.

In many parts of the country, that requires an epic journey involving planes, trains, and automobiles. But since we live in Southern California, it's less than a four-hour drive. So a year later when their church organized a weekend service trip to Ariana's neighborhood, Brad and Missy decided to pack up their minivan and head across the border. They told Anna they couldn't be sure they would meet Ariana, but it turned out that she lived right across the dirt road from the church with which they were partnering.

That was eight years ago, but Anna and Ariana are still friends. Anna's family made it a priority to visit once or twice each year, sometimes taking the lead to coordinate trips for their church. In between visits, Anna and Ariana occasionally write back and forth. The Griffins keep a picture of Anna and Ariana near their dining room table to prompt conversations about Ariana and other friends in Mexico, as well as people in the Pasadena community who live with poverty or injustice.

During one visit to Ensenada, the Griffins learned how much this relationship means to Ariana. She showed them a special photo album she keeps in her bedroom with pictures the family has sent her through the years.

The impact of this relationship spills over into the rest of the family as well. Anna's younger sister feels a special connection to Ariana, and her little brother treasures a toy car given to him by Ariana's father, Romero. Brad notes, "This family has adopted us just as much as we've adopted them."

Brad and Missy would be the first to say they don't have it all figured out. Some months they are intentional in the way they serve others, and other months they are hit by the same calendar wave that washes away everyone's good intentions. But what I love about Brad and Missy's service is that they listened to their daughter, took one faithful step at a time, and unleashed a flood of Jesus-centered ministry that continues to change both Ariana and their own family.

Sticky Findings

1 The Local Congregation Is a Service Springboard

In our interviews with fifty Sticky Faith parents, service was a theme that cut across their answers. While we had specific questions about service, the topic was also mentioned when parents were asked to describe what they did to stay connected with their kids in the midst of family busyness, what their impetus was for family faith conversations, and what kind of impact family trips and vacations had on their family. Of all the themes that emerged from the transcripts, volunteering was one of the more pervasive builders of Sticky Faith.

Frequently, a local church was the catalyst for this service. Some families found that their congregation walked with them hand in hand throughout their service journey. For other parents, such as Brad and Missy Griffin, their church provided the spark for their family, and then it was up to them to fan those flames in their kids. Either way, to our research team's delight, the majority of the parents we interviewed who were engaged with their children in serving others were grateful for their congregation's role in stoking the fire of family service.

2 Young People Want to Be Involved in Service and Justice Work

We asked the five hundred youth group graduates in our study what they wished they'd had more of in youth group. Of the thirteen options we provided, their number one answer was "time for deep conversation."

Second was "mission trips."

Third was "service projects."

Last was "games."

Admittedly, these were high school seniors. A survey of seventh-graders may have yielded a different hierarchy. Nonetheless, God has given your child or teenager a set of skills, gifts, and passions

What if my kid doesn't want to serve?

If the only service your son or daughter wants to engage in is to serve themselves another bowl of ice cream before bed, what should you do? Should you make them serve with your family, or should you abandon the service ship?

Neither of those extremes seems like the winning choice. Instead try finding a middle ground with your child by doing the following:

Give them choices. If your church or your kid's school is heavily involved in service, you might want to ask your child to choose one activity from the service menu over the next few months. The more choices you can give, the better your child's attitude is likely to be. In addition, by exposing them to a variety of experiences over the course of several years, you will increase the likelihood that they will discover a longer-lasting interest in some person or cause.

Tap into their interests. What does your child seem to care about? Do they seem passionate about environmental reform? Or are they more interested in improving the quality of education in your town? Does your child seem touched when they hear about children who are adopted or abused? Even if it's just a tiny spark, what seems to light your child's fire?

Take into account their personality and talents. A sociable child might love to interact with patrons at a soup pantry, while a quiet, artistic child might prefer making a card or writing a letter to cheer a homebound senior or missionary. A computer whiz might like to work on the church website, while a budding teacher might enjoy volunteering to teach Sunday school. Even if the service "fit" isn't quite perfect, however, your child will learn valuable information about themselves and the world around them as they serve.

Involve a friend. As with most activities, teenagers are often more interested in serving if they can bring along a friend. Even though it may require more driving and schedule juggling to add a buddy to the mix, the payoff is worth it if it will decrease your child's potential whining and complaining.

Take baby steps. Maybe the first—and best—step for your child and your family is a small step, like sending an email to a local politician or cleaning out your child's bedroom and giving an extra batch of clothes to a nearby homeless shelter.

Make it personal. Perhaps your kids don't want to serve because they don't feel personally connected to the cause. Who could you introduce to your family to give them a face-to-face connection with the people they could impact? Maybe a tour of a nearby mentoring center or a conversation with someone at your church who was formerly involved in a gang would help the service opportunity hit home.

that can be used to help others and advocate for justice.[1] At some (maybe subconscious) level, your child senses these inclinations and feels dissatisfied until they live out that divine calling.

③ Service as We're Currently Doing It Isn't Sticking Like We Would Hope

More than two million US teens participate in mission trips annually. While that's something to cheer, for five out of six of them, the trips don't make a lasting mark on their lives.[2]

Research indicates that our current service experiences might not be yielding the spiritual bang we would hope for, at least not in the long term. For example:[3]

- The explosive growth in the number of short-term mission trips among both kids and adults has *not* translated into similarly explosive growth in the number of career missionaries.

- It's not clear whether participation in service trips causes participants to give more money to alleviate poverty once they return to "normal" life.

- Service trips do not seem to reduce participants' tendencies toward materialism.

To rephrase the *Field of Dreams* mantra: If we send them, they will grow.

Perhaps.

④ Service Is More Likely to Stick When It's Not an Event but a Process

Motivated by the good news that young people want to serve, and by the bad news that we are falling far short of fostering the fruit that could be yielded from the justice vine, we at the Fuller Youth Institute have examined how families and churches can experience more Sticky service. Our research, done in collaboration with Dave Livermore of the Global Learning Center at Grand Rapids

Theological Seminary and Terry Linhart of Bethel College (Indiana), suggests that families and churches need to do a better job of walking with young people before, during, and after their mission experience.[4]

Whether you are involved in a Saturday visit to a local children's hospital or a ten-day trip to South America, we recommend an experiential education framework for your family, called the Before/During/After Model (see figure).[5]

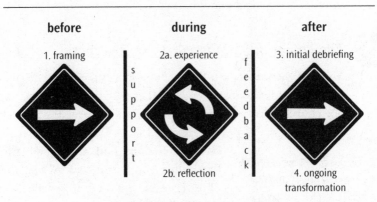

The Before/During/After Model

Step 1. Before: Framing. A lasting service experience starts when we help our children and teenagers frame the sometimes mind-blowing and other times menial experiences that await them.

Step 2. During: Experience and Reflection. The primary component of students' learning during their actual service is the cycle of experience and reflection. Even if we parents aren't physically present with our kids during their school or church service work, hopefully their adult leaders are helping them dig past their experiences to unearth deeper emotional and theological insights.

Step 3. After: Initial Debrief. The goal of the third step, the initial debriefing that occurs shortly after our sons or daughters return home, is to help them identify the changes they hope will stick long-term.

Step 4. After: Ongoing Transformation. In the fourth and final step, ongoing transformation, we parents take the next several weeks to help our kids connect the dots between the public school they painted in Philadelphia and the homeless man they pass every day on their way to school.[6]

As with many areas of family life, less is more. In view of our research, if this type of process feels overwhelming to you, we suggest you do less volunteering but more reflection and conversation in order to yield a greater harvest.

5 The Power of Families Serving Together

Much of the service our family experiences comes as the five of us serve individually instead of together. My husband is the chair of our church's deacons board. Our three kids serve through church and school. I feel called to equip teenagers with the lifelong faith they need, through the Fuller Youth Institute. When the five of us serve, we are often in separate rooms.

I wish our family would think more about others and less about ourselves. We get too bogged down with the day-to-day to think about the world as a whole.

—Bobbi

While those are valid and important ways to impact others, a unique strength comes when family members serve not solo but as a team. Motivated by her study of thirty-two congregations from diverse denominations and geographical regions in the United States, Diana Garland champions the power of family members serving together instead of separately. Not only does serving together become a scheduled activity that brings family members into the same car or room; Garland's research indicates that "serving as a team helps family members stay involved when they might not if they were serving as individuals."[7]

As one of the moms we interviewed vividly described, "While I wish this wasn't the case, when I talk with my boys about how I hope they are willing to serve the Lord, they sometimes roll their eyes. When we actually serve the Lord together as a family, they never roll their eyes."

Sticky Ideas

Rice and Bean Sunday Dinner

Bryan and Sharla wanted to give their kids a taste of what it's like to scrimp on food. Together with their twelve-year-old and their ten-year-old, they came up with the idea of "Rice and Bean Sunday Dinner." Every Sunday night, they have white rice and pinto beans.

Every Sunday.

Sometimes they add the luxury of salsa, cheese, or sour cream. Regardless of whether they add toppings to the meal, the family donates the money they would have spent on a more elaborate Sunday dinner to a ministry that feeds poor people in their city. They take time during each Sunday meal to talk about people they know who are struggling financially, as well as current events that revolve around poverty in other countries.

> *Our church has partnered with a foundation that's fighting poverty in Haiti. As a family, we agreed to make a collective sacrifice to sponsor a Haitian child. So every Tuesday night, we have eggs and toast for dinner. Our kids actually love it.*
>
> —Dana

Their favorite method of cooking the beans and rice is to throw them in the crock-pot on Sunday morning. So not only are they experiencing the way that much of the world eats, and donating money to people in need; they have a more relaxing Sabbath because their dinner is taken care of.

Your Family

- What might happen if one day you modified a meal, or even dessert or drinks at a meal, to give your family a sense of what much of the world experiences?

- What might happen in your family if that one-time experiment turned into a regular practice?

"You're Fifteen ... Time to Go on a Short-Term Mission Trip"

Wanting to combine Sticky Faith service with a one-on-one ritual for each of his four kids, Garrett decided that in the year each child turned fifteen, he'd take him or her on a seven- to ten-day short-term mission trip. Luckily for Garrett, his church was committed to short-term missions and took multiple groups on cross-cultural service adventures. With one child at a time, Garrett has done father-child short-term trips to Panama, Namibia, Brazil, and Ukraine.

Before each trip, Garrett and his son or daughter researched the cultural context of the country they would be visiting and discussed Scripture passages they hoped would guide their justice work. After they returned, they tried to hold each other accountable for changes they sensed God wanted them to make in their own lives.

Now that all four kids have graduated from high school, Garrett reflected in our interview with him: "Those trips were an important tradition in our family. They solidified our kids' relationships with God and with me."

Your Family

- How could service become a tradition your kids look forward to?
- If one-on-one trips with each of your kids aren't feasible, what would be realistic for your family?

Create Your Own Bread Line

Eduardo and Teresa's church isn't involved in ministry to the homeless, but that doesn't mean their family can't be. Feeling nudged by God to engage in conversation with homeless folks, Eduardo and Teresa regularly make more than a hundred sandwiches with their second-grader and preschooler. The four of them create their own kitchen assembly line complete with ham, cheese, and bread. Then they head to the downtown rescue mission and stand alongside its staff to distribute the food.

It may be the sight of an adorable five-year-old handing out a sandwich, or it may be the prospect of ham and cheese on sourdough, but for whatever reason, Eduardo and Teresa find that the men, women, and children they meet are open to having short conversations. Eduardo and Teresa are hoping that these interactions are helping their young children grasp that all people deserve to be nourished and treated with dignity.

Your Family

- How often does your family see homeless people?
- What are you teaching your kids about justice and homelessness by the way you respond to those folks?

Missionary Sleepovers

John and Dena don't have a huge home, but they have a huge heart for long-term missionaries serving around the world. They have told their church that if a missionary needs a place to stay—whether it be for one night or one month—they are open to hosting them. They want their home to be a refuge and a blessing to weary missionaries and their families.

Over breakfasts and dinners, John and Dena's two elementary-age children hear the adults discussing what God is doing around the world. Ahead of these meals, John and Dena try to brainstorm with their kids about the questions they could ask their guests so that all generations are part of the conversation. Admittedly, their kids don't always love having to share a bedroom so the missionaries can have a room to themselves, but John and Dena feel that's a small price to pay for the privilege of having people who are involved in God's work in the world enjoying dessert in their dining room.

Your Family

- How could your home be used by God to refresh people in full-time vocational ministry and simultaneously impact your family?

- Regardless of the size of your home and how you feel about having guests stay overnight, what local ministry or church leader could you invite over who could stimulate an interesting dinner conversation for your family?

Code Word "Salt"

Wanting to give their two teenagers a biblically rooted theology, Jeremy and Janna have explained that their family serves others as a way to live out Jesus' declaration in Matthew 5:13 that his followers are the salt of the earth. Sometimes the family chooses to be "salt" by making cookies or buying flowers for someone who is struggling.

Other times the family decides that being "salt" means a greater sacrifice, like cleaning a friend's car or even cleaning an entire house. When their kids would rather skip out on these service activities, Jeremy and Janna remind them that "it's a salt thing." Periodically the kids return the favor by reminding Jeremy and Janna that "it's a salt thing" when their parents would rather opt for what's convenient than what's right.

Your Family

- What Scripture verses motivate you to serve others?

- How could you help your kids understand what these verses mean to you, as well as to them?

Missionary Mail

At least once a month, a missionary enters the home of the Bowman family. Not in the form of a walking and talking human but in the form of prayer letters from missionaries whom the Bowmans support.

Wanting to leverage these letters, Jon and Gina Bowman have decided to do more than scan and recycle them. They share the letters, and emails from the missionaries as well, with their kids over meals or during car rides, and then they all pray together for the needs the missionaries mention. Eventually the Bowmans hope to take their kids on an overseas mission trip. In the meantime, they are grateful for the missionary mail and email that flatten the world and help their family participate in God's work across several continents.

> My stepdaughter knew a girl at school whose dad had lost his job, so our small group decided to anonymously buy her school lunches for a year. I asked our stepdaughter not to tell anyone what we had done, and she didn't. But I'm glad she knows that our family steps in to help others, and even mobilizes others to get involved too.
>
> —Vic

Your Family

- How connected are your kids with the missionaries or ministry leaders whom your family financially supports?

- What could you do to help your kids understand this slice of your family's financial stewardship and feel more relationally engaged with people you are supporting?

Buy a Christmas Cow

For several Decembers in a row, Billy and Chrissy sat with their three kids at the dining room table, looked through a catalog, and chose Christmas gifts for families around the world. This was no ordinary catalog; these were gifts provided by a ministry that could forever change the financial situation of folks trapped in poverty. A cow could give a family in Uganda the chance to sell milk to neighbors; a sheep could provide wool blankets that could be traded for food and education in Kenya.

These gifts were the quintessential "gifts that keep on giving."

While Billy and Chrissy loved this tradition, they felt their kids weren't truly owning the experience. Since it was always Mom and Dad's money that was being spent, the twenty-minute discussions over the catalog options were quickly forgotten.

So three years ago Billy and Chrissy decided to give their kids a chance to earn the money to buy these unique Christmas gifts. Their kids can now earn gift money by doing work that goes above and beyond their regular chores, such as washing windows, cleaning out the refrigerator, or power-spraying the back patio. Billy and Chrissy have found that their kids take the discussion more seriously when it's their time and sweat that secured the funds needed for that special Christmas cow.

Your Family

- When, if at all, do your kids devote their time and effort to earn money that helps others?
- If not at Christmastime, when is a logical season for you to encourage your kids to earn some extra money to change someone else's life?

 ## Stacking the Church Chairs

Many of the parents we interviewed find rich opportunities for their family to volunteer together during their congregation's weekend worship services. Whether the opportunities involve serving on the tech team that controls lighting and slides or teaching third-grade Sunday school every month, parents relish the chance to work alongside their kids. And this kind of service doesn't involve much extra time or hassle.

Ryan and Amberly have made this "serve where we are" ethic part of their family identity. As they explain, "We've told our kids that we all are going to set up and tear down chairs together at church. This is who we are as a family. This is what we do. It's kind of a joke that we're always the last ones to leave because we don't leave until everything is cleaned up and put away."

Your Family

- What opportunities are there for you to serve with your kids in your church?

- Is it important to you to make serving others part of your family identity? If so, what changes might you want to make so your kids grasp that this is who you are?

Twenty-Dollar Service Adventure

Greg and Hannah are tight on money, but they are always looking for creative ways to bless others, even if all they have is a few dollars. Wanting to help their kids develop a vision for service, they put twenty dollars in a handful of envelopes and then stashed those envelopes in their cars, Hannah's purse, and their living room.

They told their kids, "That twenty dollars is for us to use to help others. Let's see how creative we can be with the money." When an envelope is empty, Greg and Hannah replenish it with another twenty dollars.

As you might imagine, much of the envelope money has been used to buy meals for homeless folks. But the family has also lavishly tipped waiters and waitresses at their favorite restaurants who were short on rent money. The kids have given extra money toward the bicycle their middle school ministry was trying to buy for a missionary in Cambodia. They even once brought a fruit smoothie to their school principal, knowing he was distraught over pending budget cuts.

Greg and Hannah and their kids discovered that a handful of twenty-dollar bills can make a difference in other people's lives, as well as in their own family.

Your Family

- How could a little bit of cash be a catalyst for blessing others?
- In addition to some cash, what other resources does your family have that could be used to serve and help others?
- As you bless others, how do you think your own family will be blessed?

Our Family's Steps toward Sticky Faith

Take a few moments on your own, or with your spouse, your friends, or your small group, to reflect on some potential next steps toward Sticky Faith.

Sticky Findings

On a scale of 1 to 5 (with 1 being "we stink at this" and 5 being "we rock at this"), rate your family on the research findings presented in this chapter.

1| We take advantage of the service opportunities provided by our church.

① ② ③ ④ ⑤

2| I can identify my kids' God-given passions and gifts that can be used to serve others.

① ② ③ ④ ⑤

3| We view service not as an event but as a process that we talk about before, during, and after our service experiences.

① ② ③ ④ ⑤

4| Our family serves together, not just separately.

① ② ③ ④ ⑤

Sticky Ideas

1| In what ways has serving and blessing others already enriched your family's relationships and faith?

2| Given your ranking of the findings in the previous section, as well as the ideas you've read in this chapter, what one or two changes might you want to make in your family?

3| What can you do in the next few weeks or month to move toward these changes?

Chapter 12

Sticky Transitions

Helping Kids Leave Home with a Faith of Their Own

The two credit card applications I expected. The handwritten letter was a surprise.

It was my first day on campus as a college freshman. With the help of my parents and two RAs, all of my belongings had been carried from my Toyota to my dorm room that morning. I had unpacked my clothes, plugged in my Macintosh computer (a light-gray tower about the size of three cereal boxes), spread out my new blue and white bedspread, and strategically placed my Bible on a visible but not too obvious shelf above my desk.

About the time I was wondering what to do next, my roommate walked in. I immediately liked Tammy. Not only was she cheerful and friendly, but she was also a Christian (a rarity at my college) who was taller than me (I'm six feet tall, so that's even more of a rarity). A few other freshmen on our floor swung by our room and asked us if we wanted to walk a few blocks with them to check our PO boxes. Not having anything pressing to do and wanting to get to know our floor-mates, Tammy and I agreed.

Upon opening my PO box, I immediately discarded the two credit card brochures. My mom had warned me about those. While I didn't know much about money, I knew I didn't want to drown in credit card debt.

As I chucked the applications, I was surprised to find a handwritten note. It was from Pamela, one of the high school small group leaders in my home church. The week before I had packed up my car for the drive to college, Pamela had asked my mom for the address to my PO box. She wasn't even my small group leader, but she knew enough about life at college that she wanted a cheerful greeting from home to be waiting for me.

I walked back to my dorm room and taped that note from Pamela to the right of my mirror. Her note stayed there until Christmas, a daily reminder that my home church was thinking about me and praying for me. I had not been forgotten.

In the twenty-five years since I opened my PO box, technology has expanded the quantity and quality of pipes we can use to shower high school graduates with our care and concern. Our research team recently heard from Sheila, a mom who asked a number of her church friends to write to her son Matthew, who was heading to a college fifteen hundred miles from home. A week later Matthew posted on Facebook, "I've only been at college for a week, and I have already received countless letters, texts, and posts from my home church. Thank you all so much! Every letter has encouraged me to keep my faith strong. With all the 'options' out there at college, it's comforting to know that I have a church family back home supporting me and my beliefs. If you haven't written to a college student yet, I encourage you to do so. It will make their day!"

To Sheila's delight, Matthew received letters from folks she hadn't directly asked to write him. Upon hearing from others about her invitation, they had decided to pick up a pen to let Matthew know that while he was out of sight, he wasn't out of mind.

Sticky Findings

1 **_Reach Out and Stay in Touch with Someone_**

Pamela's note to me and Sheila's mail bombardment for her son are more than just fun ideas; they are actually faith-building. Our Sticky Faith study of youth group graduates indicates that contact from at least one adult from the congregation outside of the youth ministry during the first semester of college is linked to faith maturity. Whether it's through newer technology like texting or something you've perhaps heard of called the US Postal Service, adults who keep in touch with your emerging-adult child send faith-building messages that can still be reverberating three years later.[1]

2 Avoid the Silent Treatment

The last several years have revealed a tendency among many parents to overparent. In a practice commonly referred to as "helicopter parenting," parents will often take too much initiative in relationship with their child and in shouldering responsibilities that could and should be borne by their maturing child. Iconic examples of helicopter parenting include parents who contact professors to complain about a grade their college-age child has received, or parents who communicate with a child's potential employer during the job interview process.

Multiple studies indicate that helicopter parenting can hinder an emerging adult's maturation. The more that emerging adults feel controlled by their parents, the more difficulties they experience in establishing committed choices. Even more discouraging, emerging adults who feel overparented are less likely to identify with or feel certain about choices they *do* make.[2] In her book *A Nation of Wimps*, Hara Estroff Marano describes the psychological effects of parental interference: "Intrusive parenting undermines children in the most fundamental ways. It spawns anxious attachment in the children, setting them up for lifelong fragility."[3]

In an effort to avoid helicopter parenting, many parents are tempted to swing to the other extreme. They give their kids excessive space when they head to college, by "observing radio silence." Our research indicates that this lack of communication can damage young people's faith. Regardless of whether the student or the parent initiated the contact, and regardless of whether the communication was by phone, email, or text, there is a positive relationship between a student's ongoing contact with their parents and their emotional and practical adjustment to college.

3 From a Cruise Ship to a Dinghy

The vast majority of seniors—six out of seven—say they are not prepared for what they will face after they graduate. As one first-year college student vividly described, "Transitioning out of high school into college is like you're leaving on a giant cruise ship from this harbor and everyone is waving you off. This ship is your faith, but as soon as you start sailing out to this port called college, you realize you're in a dinghy. You're not prepared, and your boat is sinking."

Our research indicates that for students there is a link between feeling prepared and having a thriving faith. So when students don't feel set up for success in their transition to college, their faith may suffer.

4 Failing to Find Church

The good news for college freshmen living away from home is that getting connected with either a church or an on-campus ministry is linked to Sticky Faith.

Now comes the bad news. During the fall of freshman year, only 40 percent of the youth group graduates we studied were attending an on-campus fellowship once a week or more. Slightly

---

Does it matter whether my child goes to a Christian high school or a Christian college?

This is a great question, and it's one we're often asked. Answering that question wasn't a primary goal of our study, so we didn't recruit the right ratios of students to address what type of high school (public, non-faith-based private, Christian, or home school) or college (public, non-faith-based private, or Christian) was most closely correlated with Sticky Faith. What we have learned in our ongoing discussions with students and parents is that each type of school has its faith challenges. Regardless of the type of school, we encourage young people to get plugged into a supportive, Christ-centered group of friends as soon as possible.

---

more encouraging, approximately 57 percent of youth group graduates were attending church once a week or more.

Perhaps the percentage of students engaged in a college ministry or church isn't higher because youth group graduates lack the tools to get plugged in. Less than 40 percent of graduating seniors feel prepared to find a new church. Finding a church was one of youth group graduates' top three difficulties in transitioning to college.

5 Managing Daily Life Is Overwhelming

In his study of college freshmen, sociologist Tim Clydesdale found that students often become stunned by all they have to tackle in their "daily life management." Away from parents and the stability of home, young people can be somewhat shell-shocked by the lack of boundaries and the abundance of new choices. Add to that emotional roller coaster the additional pressures of finances, schoolwork, meals, and even laundry, and many students are fighting hard just to physically and emotionally survive. For those students consumed with basic survival, pouring energy into faith development is a bridge too far.[4]

Our own research seems to confirm this preoccupation with daily life management. Nearly half of the college freshmen we surveyed felt anxious that so much was suddenly up to them to decide. Interestingly, the students we surveyed found two areas especially challenging for their faith integration: time (they now spend far less time in class than they did in high school) and money (creating challenges for freshmen who are greeted by enticing credit card applications, as I was).

6 The First Two Weeks = the Next Few Years

A common theme in students' descriptions of their college experience is the importance of their first two weeks. It is during those first fourteen days that students make key decisions about sex, drinking, and other high-risk behaviors as well as about allegiance to a local church or on-campus ministry. The decisions they make during those two weeks can set them on a trajectory that lasts for the rest of their college experience.

As we have shared that trend with college pastors and college parachurch leaders, they have often responded that it's not really a two-week window. It's a four-day window. The decisions students make in the first four days set them on a path they will likely follow for the next four years.

Sticky Ideas

 ## *Preparing for College*

Given the data about the first two weeks of college—and even the first four days—wise parents help their young-adult child envision and prepare for their new lifestyle as well as develop a plan for those key early days. Whether their college-bound child is staying at home for school or moving away, they try to discuss the following questions with them.

- Where will you be living? How will that affect your friendships?
- What church or on-campus ministry will you join?
- What will your class load be?
- When will you study and do your homework?
- What extracurricular activities interest you? How much time will that involve?
- How much time can you devote to a job?
- What is your budget for school expenses? For personal expenses?
- What will you do when someone invites you to a party?
- If you decide to go to a party, what will you drink?
- What kind of person will you date? How will you learn about that person's character?

- Where will you go for help if you are struggling academically, physically, emotionally, practically, or relationally?
- What can you do those first few days and weeks to connect with God?
- How much communication do you want to have with your family those first days and weeks?

If the flavor of your relationship with your child means that talking over these questions would feel forced or awkward, don't discard them. With your child, identify another caring adult conversation partner to help them develop a vision and plan for those pivotal first days.

Your Family

- Which of these questions is most important for you to discuss with your child?
- What additional questions that aren't on the list do you need to talk over with them?
- If you aren't the person to have this conversation, which adult would you hope can discuss these questions with your child?

How can I help my child transition to the job force and independence?

While much of this Sticky Faith guide unpacks our research on young people headed to college, at some point those same young people will graduate from college (hopefully) and find employment (double hopefully). Plus, many young people head straight to the workforce after high school.

As we have talked with parents eager to support their emerging adult's transition to the job force, three questions repeatedly surface. We asked one of our FYI Advisory Council members, Steve Argue, who serves as a pastor and theologian in residence at Mars Hill Bible Church in Grand Rapids, Michigan, to share his best answers to those questions.

I'm hearing more about students taking a "gap year." Why are students doing this, and how can I help my child make sure it's a gap year and not a gap decade?

More emerging adults are opting to take a year to work, serve, or travel before heading to college. Many need the break, don't know what they want to study, or are seeking a bit of adventure. The parents I have talked with who have been successful in helping their children go this route have established clear on-ramps and off-ramps for this experience. In other words, with their emerging adult, they have mapped out plans before and *after* their gap year experience. You do not want the gap year to turn into gap *years*, delaying the important next steps that young adults need to take toward education and career.

The job market is tough these days for all young people, including my child. How can I support my child without putting undue pressure on them to find a job?

It's not easy for young people to transition to the job force today. They're regularly accused of being lazy or feeling they're entitled, but often the reality is that emerging adults are competing against a large number of applicants worldwide, including older workers who cannot yet retire. While you may assume that asking questions about the job search is a way to encourage your child, they may read that as pressure and lack of trust. So talk with your child about how you can best support them, and when. Let your child know you're available to talk with them and pray for them. And encourage them to articulate their needs with you. That is, in itself, an important part of growing up.

My child is working but doesn't make enough to rent their own place. Even if they live with me at home for a while, how can I prepare them for eventually living on their own?

Whether your child chooses to go to school or work while living at home, or returns home between semesters or after college, it's important that you define the new relationship you have with your emerging adult. It's too easy for all of you to default back to old parent-child relationships that don't prepare them (or you) for the future. So make sure you establish clear guidelines for what it means to live together—how you respect each other's schedules, share household chores, handle rent, deal with having friends over, and so on. Check with each other on a regular basis (monthly or quarterly) to revisit these mutually established expectations. This provides opportunity for constructive feedback and may prevent arguments. Further, help them with longer-term skills, like keeping a budget and saving for future goals. Odds are good you should refrain from getting too involved in the personal choices they are making (friends, use of time, priorities, and so on), unless they ask for your input. However, if their choices affect you, then it's important that you remind them of your expectations. In some cases, you may even want to establish a timeline for their moving out on their own and help them work toward that goal.

"Take a Senior to Church" Day

Realizing that their family's home church was all his son knew, Curtis decided to take his son, who would soon be graduating from high school, on a handful of Sunday field trips to churches near where they lived. No, they weren't church hopping. Instead they were visiting unfamiliar churches so Curtis's son could experience what it feels like to walk into a new church, worship with a new music team, and learn from a new lead pastor.

Every weekend after visiting a new church, Curtis and his son would go out to lunch to debrief what they had experienced. They talked about their impressions of the worship service, what they appreciated about the church, and what they wished were different. Curtis's hope was that these field trips with his son would increase the odds that after the young man left home, he would visit a few churches on his own until he found one that felt right.

Your Family

- What are you doing to prepare your child to find a new church?
- How would visiting the worship services of some local churches perhaps predispose your child to do likewise after they move away from home?

On-Campus Ministry Connection

Since God had used on-campus ministries to deepen both Danny's and Cindy's faith in college, they wanted their children to be exposed to parachurch campus ministries as a vibrant Sticky Faith option. Once each of their children chose their college, Danny and Cindy took them on a tour of that college during their senior year. Not only did they visit the library, dorms, and classrooms, but they also scheduled the dates of the trip to align with the large group meeting of a dynamic on-campus ministry.

When possible, Danny and Cindy contacted a staff member (often an intern) of that ministry ahead of time and invited them to dinner prior to the large group fellowship. That way they and their child could ask all sorts of questions about the ministry. As a bonus, their child usually ended up sitting with that staff person at the large group gathering (which was way more hip than sitting with Mom and Dad) and was introduced to a number of students who were already involved.

As Cindy summarized, "Visiting an on-campus ministry often meant we had to spend one additional night on campus, which translated into more money for a hotel room. But it was so worth it, because our child knew where and when that ministry met. More importantly, they knew some of the staff and students who were already involved."

Your Family

- As you think about visiting potential college campuses, or the college campus your child ends up choosing, how big of a priority should you place on visiting on-campus ministries?

- What are the schedule and budget ramifications of your answer to the first question?

Interviewing College Students in Front of Your Kids

When we asked Lynnea, a mom of three current college students, how she prepared her daughters for life in college, her answer was simple: "I basically interviewed college students in front of them. I invited college students from our church over for dinner and asked them questions in front of my girls, like, How did you handle the pressures of alcohol? or, How did you try to make good dating choices? Indirect communication seemed to be the best way to get through to my girls."

Lynnea's daughters knew what she was up to, but since her daughters were going to hear it from someone, they seemed to prefer advice from young adults who were a few years older than them instead of advice from Mom.

Your Family

- What young people do your kids look up to who you think have made good choices in college?
- How could you involve them in the discussions you want to have with your kids about life after high school?

What if my child is headed into the military after graduation?

Each year, families send off high school graduates to serve in the military. While much of our research at FYI has been focused on Sticky Faith in college and beyond, we are aware of the need to explore how faith can be nurtured for graduates who head off to serve in one of the armed forces.[*]

FYI Advisory Council member Mark Maines serves as a Marine Corps chaplain, currently assigned to a USMC infantry battalion. We recently asked Mark to describe the unique Sticky Faith issues facing military personnel and their families.

What does Sticky Faith look like for a new military member? What are some of the common features you have seen among people whose faith seems to survive the transition well?

Connecting to a faith community is monumental in helping faith stick in this environment. Marines, soldiers, and sailors are warriors. They pride themselves on being the "first to fight," and they are the best in the world at it. They are trained to be at war, so

when service members are in garrison (a noncombat or training environment), we pay particularly close attention to the command climate because this is the environment in which they are more likely to make poor decisions. This is what makes connecting to a community of likeminded people (even just two or three others) so important. The service members whose faith seems to be thriving are usually those who have connected with other service members who take their faith seriously.

What else have you seen that helps faith stick for high school graduates entering the military?

The presence of a mentor also makes a remarkable difference in service members' lives. In the particular battalion I serve, which supports about 1,300 marines, there is a strong mentorship program that covers everything from core values, physical fitness, and financial well-being to marital wholeness and spiritual vitality. Our primary goal is to shape them into better marines and better citizens of America, but a secondary effect of this mentoring effort is that it lowers negative behaviors across the battalion. Simply stated, fewer marines do fewer bad things when leadership engages a strong mentoring program.

What are some of the most common struggles you see among young service members? How do you see these struggles affecting their faith?

The military reflects society as a whole. So any struggle that exists outside of the military certainly exists inside of it. Alcohol abuse, drug use, and sexual abuse are all everyday issues. It's no secret that the military can be a harsh environment.

Perhaps the most serious struggle currently facing service members is the tension between taking life and valuing their own. According to data collected by the Community Counseling and Prevention Services for the Marine Corps, in 2012, 179 marines attempted suicide and forty-eight actually did commit suicide.[**] Although Marine Corps leadership is taking proactive action, we still have yet to determine how to best reach out to marines and sailors who are thinking about harming themselves.

When a service member returns home, what should parents do?

Depending on where this person was deployed, parents have to acknowledge that the person now standing in front of them is not the same individual who left home. Military service changes you. Deployments change you. War inevitably changes you. However, we often do not know how or to what extent. We need to create the kind of relational space where service members are allowed to be who they have become.

Henri Nouwen writes powerfully, "Hospitality ... means primarily the creation of a free space where the stranger can enter and become a friend instead of an enemy. Hospitality is not to change people, but to offer them space where change can take place."[***] We need to be willing to hear these young people's stories. We need to engage, to inquire, to listen without judgment, and to welcome them back to a truly hospitable home. We may be proud of their service, but I think it is more important to truly understand *how* they served. Returning service members need to tell their story, and we need to hear the stories they tell.

---

* This sidebar is adapted from an *FYI E-Journal* article titled "Sticky Faith Deployed: Helping Students Prepare Faith for Military Service," *http://stickyfaith.org/articles/sticky-faith-deployed*.

** Adam Walsh, "Marine and Family Program Prevention Services Update July 2013," slide presentation by the Community Counseling and Prevention Services Headquarters, Marine Corps.

*** Henri J. M. Nouwen, *Reaching Out* (New York: Doubleday, 1986), 71.

This Is How a Washing Machine Works

Sprinkled throughout the responses to our interview question about the transition out of the home were wise parents' accounts of their efforts to prepare their kids for adulthood not only spiritually and emotionally but also logistically. Before their kids left home (or were granted more "adult" independence, for those who stayed home after graduation), they made sure their kids knew how to

- do laundry
- do dishes and basic housecleaning tasks
- use an ATM machine
- write a check
- conduct online banking
- perform basic first aid
- hang a picture (a skill that many college freshmen lack but almost all need)
- grocery shop with a budget
- cook a few simple meals
- understand routine car maintenance and access emergency road service
- utilize public transportation

Your Family

- Leaving aside spiritual and emotional preparation for a moment, how prepared is your child to handle the logistics of life after high school?
- What two skills would you like to teach your child this next month?

Full Freedom for Not-Quite College Students

Desiree, a mom of three young adult sons, prepared her sons for life after high school by treating them like college students *during twelfth grade*. What did this look like? Desiree and her husband,

Oscar, made two major changes. First, they eliminated as many rules as possible. Second, they shifted the responsibility for making wise choices from their shoulders to their sons'.

Instead of a curfew, the boys told their parents when they wanted to be home. If they were going to deviate from that significantly, they needed to call home and let their parents know.

It was up to the boys to figure out how to balance homework, friendships, and jobs.

It was up to the boys to figure out how long to sleep in on Saturday morning, given what they needed to get done that weekend.

While Desiree and Oscar relinquished some rules, they never relinquished their relationship with their sons. They remained relationally involved and connected, available for conversation and input whenever the boys wanted.

Did the boys make some mistakes? You bet. But Desiree was glad that she and Oscar were there to help them learn from their mistakes while the stakes were relatively low, instead of after graduation when the stakes grow higher.

Your Family

- How can you give your kids more opportunities to make their own choices—and fail—while you're still around to help pick up the pieces from any mistakes they might make?

- If Desiree's plan feels like too much freedom for your kids, would it make sense for your children when they are high school seniors to have a weekend, or a week or two, during which you treat them like college students?

 ### Sundae for Your Senior

After hearing about our research on high school seniors, Craig and Sherri decided to do a special "starting college ceremony" for Annika, their soon-to-be college freshman daughter. The summer before she headed to the local junior college was so hectic for Annika that they almost punted on the idea, but they figured that they had enough time and energy to pull together a simple one-hour dessert with five adults who had been especially significant to her.

Ahead of time, they asked these five folks to write a blessing or Scripture passage for Annika on an index card and send that card, along with a photo of themselves, to Craig and Sherri.

The night of the sundae dessert, all of the adults as well as Annika's entire family (including four younger siblings) sat in a circle. The adults shared their words of advice, blessing, and Scripture for Annika, and then each prayed over her. Before leaving, the adults committed to keep in touch with her as she started this new chapter of her life. Using an online photo album service, Craig later created a memory book of that night, including the five adults' words of encouragement, for Annika to take with her.

While Craig and Sherri realize there are no faith guarantees, they are sure of this: Annika knows that they and five other amazing adults are there for her to help her when her faith flounders.

Your Family

- What adults can you involve in some sort of graduation or send-off event?
- If a gathering doesn't fit your family, what adults could share some meaningful advice that you could compile and present to your child?

 ## A Plan for When You Fail

Normally an optimist, Art knew that while his daughter, Amanda, generally made good choices, it was only a matter of time before she made a choice that she'd regret. Amanda had decided to do a gap year after high school, meaning she had delayed heading to college for a year and was living at home. Although much of her life was familiar, many of her closest friends were going away to school, leaving Amanda on her own to find new friends. It didn't help that while their church had a thriving high school ministry, the college ministry there was rather anemic. Given Amanda's stage in life, as well as the sin nature we all struggle with, Art knew it wasn't a matter of if she would flounder or fail, but when.

So right around the time Amanda graduated, Art took her out for coffee and asked her a few questions:

- When you flounder or fail, what wise friend or adult will you talk to?

- What Scripture verses do you think will be especially helpful?

- How can your mom and I help you in the midst of your struggles?

Art knew that he couldn't prevent Amanda from stumbling, but when she did, he wanted her to have a plan to dust herself off and continue her faith journey.

Your Family

- What can you do to prepare your student to recover after a moral or personal failure?

- How might staying at home after high school graduation be helpful for a young person's faith development? How might it be challenging?

Our Family's Steps toward Sticky Faith

Take a few moments on your own, or with your spouse, your friends, or your small group, to reflect on some potential next steps toward Sticky Faith.

Sticky Findings

On a scale of 1 to 5 (with 1 being "we stink at this" and 5 being "we rock at this"), rate your family on the research findings presented in this chapter.

1| My child would say they are very prepared for life after high school.

① ② ③ ④ ⑤

2| I can name at least five adults who would keep in touch with my child after graduation if I asked them to.

① ② ③ ④ ⑤

3| My child knows how to connect with a church or on-campus ministry after graduation.

① ② ③ ④ ⑤

4| My child can successfully navigate the tasks involved in daily life management after high school.

① ② ③ ④ ⑤

5| My child has a plan for the first four days in their new environment.

① ② ③ ④ ⑤

Sticky Ideas

1| If your child is in high school, what elements in your family or church are already preparing them for life after graduation?

2| Given your ranking of the findings in the previous section, as well as the ideas you've read in this chapter, what one or two changes might you want to make in your family?

3| What can you do in the next few weeks or month to move toward these changes?

Chapter 13

Taking the Next
Sticky Faith Steps
with Your Family

Have you ever watched an exercise show on TV ... while sitting on your couch, eating ice cream?

Or researched online to find out more about healthy dinners for your family, but then fed your kids hot dogs and macaroni and cheese (adding baby carrots on the side to inject some nutrition into the meal)?

Or read a magazine article praising the virtues of low-flow showerheads and then stood under an old showerhead that drenched not just you but also your entire shower stall?

I've done every single one of these things. In each case, I wanted to get in shape or eat more nutritionally or be more environmentally conscious. I had worthy goals, but I didn't know how to convert those goals into feasible, sustainable next steps.

I was full of inspiration; what I lacked was implementation.

At this point in this guide, you hopefully have a vision for your family's future. What you need is a strategy that translates that vision into concrete actions for this Thursday's dinner or next Tuesday's ride to school.

But this strategy will be unique to your family. The paths carved out by the families in this Sticky Faith guide are as varied as the families themselves. In the midst of wanting to be more intentional and learn from the ideas of other families, celebrate what is special about your family.

If you want to move from Sticky Faith rhetoric to Sticky Faith reality, we recommend that you create your own road map using the following path.

Celebrate your family's Sticky Faith practices up to this point. What practices were you already following even before you read this book? Perhaps you didn't realize until now how beneficial those practices were. Recognize what you've done well. Record those practices here:

Review your notes at the end of every chapter. Whether you read this guide on a plane flight, during a weekend, or over the course of several months, you've covered a lot of paragraph territory. Odds are good you've forgotten some of your early insights and convictions, so flip to the end of each chapter to see the findings and ideas you noted as having the most potential for your family.

If you're married, discuss those highlights with your spouse. You'll make more Sticky Faith progress if you both read this guide, but if that's not possible, share with your spouse what most impacted you. You might even ask them to read certain pages or chapters themselves so they can at least get a CliffsNotes version of what might be most relevant for your family. If you aren't married, do the same with a close family member or friend who knows you and your kids well.

What if my spouse isn't a Christian? Or what if they are a Christian but don't want to be very involved in helping build Sticky Faith?

It's impossible for you and your spouse to care equally about all things. You might value keeping the house clean, while your husband is fine with a bit of clutter. Or you might care deeply about being five minutes early to family events, while your wife views anything less than showing up ten minutes late as being on time.

Every day, you navigate areas in your marriage in which you have different levels of interest. It's not unusual for Sticky Faith to fall into that category. Instead of nagging or criticizing your spouse (which, as you've probably seen in other areas of your marriage, doesn't yield great results), try involving them through a feasible baby step.

If your spouse doesn't want to read this whole book, see if they'd be open to reading a chapter. (Depending on your kids' ages, we'd suggest chapter 4, 5, 6, or 8.)

If a chapter is a bridge too far, see if you can read them five ideas that you think could be most helpful to your family.

If five ideas seem like too many, choose your single favorite.

If they're not even interested in hearing one idea, that doesn't mean you abdicate altogether your hopes for Sticky Faith. Choose some low-hanging fruit—meaning one or two ideas that you can implement on your own, without spousal support—to gain some momentum.

We realize it's not going to be easy. A significant discrepancy between your and your spouse's commitment to building Sticky Faith may stem from a significant difference in your commitment to following Jesus Christ. Instead of a faith partnership, you may feel you're shouldering most—or maybe all—of the spiritual direction of your household. Sticky Faith might be one more area in which you feel spiritually and emotionally alone in your family.

The good news is that the church itself is a family—the family of God. Even though my husband is as (and some days more) committed to Sticky Faith as I am, we need our church and our extended family. Other caring believers lift up our weary parenting arms and speak into our kids' lives when for some reason we just can't. You might feel alone in your nuclear family, but you and your kids can turn to your extended church family and allow them to fill your emotional and spiritual tanks and travel down the Sticky Faith road with you.

Choose five ideas to try—for now. We're serious about this limit. If you choose more than five, you're more likely to fail. Five is doable. Two might perhaps be better. One idea that you pursue wholeheartedly might even be best. You can always add more ideas later. The Sticky Faith parenting race is a marathon, not a sprint.

I think my top five (or fewer) Sticky Faith ideas for our family might be:

If appropriate, talk about those ideas with your kids. Depending on your kids' ages and the nature of the ideas, it's often wise to discuss those ideas with your kids. When it comes to bringing about change in any system, we have found that people are more likely to support what they create. If you give your kids the chance to help steer your new family traditions or practices, they will be more likely to get on board.

Identify the next steps to take in the next week and month. Figure out the days and times when you will try out your ideas. If any preparation is required, mark that on your calendar or on the appropriate "to do" list or app.

Some next steps in the next week and month might be:

Post your plan in a public place. Visibility increases ongoing vision. Whether you place your ideas and next steps on an index card on your car's dashboard or on your family bulletin board, you need reminders of the Sticky Faith changes you'd like to explore.

View everything as an experiment. We at the Fuller Youth Institute know kids, but we don't know *your* kids. We know families, but we don't know *your* family. Some of the ideas that are home runs for one family might be a strikeout for yours. If what you first try flops, you may want to give it a second try, or you might want to abandon ship and try something else. Hold your general commitment to building Sticky Faith tightly, but hold the specific ideas you try lightly.

Tell a friend about your plan. Expression deepens impression. The more you share your ideas with others, the more you will tend to own them yourself. Plus, you might inspire a friend to conduct a few Sticky Faith experiments in their own family. If you feel comfortable, ask your friend to hold you accountable for the next steps you've planned.

If you're in a small group or Bible study, share your ideas at your next meeting. You might even want to suggest that your entire group read part or all of this guide so that you can support each other in your Sticky Faith journey.

One or more friends I'd like to discuss my Sticky Faith plan with are:

Schedule on your calendar when you will evaluate your idea. Depending on the time frame you've created for your next steps, mark a specific day on your calendar for you to evaluate your ideas. Whether you do this alone or with your spouse, you might also want to reread portions of this guide to help fuel your family's Sticky Faith fire.

Relax and enjoy the journey. Often when we present these findings and ideas to parents, parents tense up because they feel either over-whelmed at what lies ahead or guilty for their mistakes. As we discussed in chapter 3, Jesus is bigger than our parenting mistakes. God loves our kids even more than we do, and we can trust him with our family's faith journey.

Keep in touch with us and learn from other parents. The best idea for your family might come not from this book but from an online portal we've created for parents to journey together and sharpen each other. So visit *stickyfaith.org* to sign up for our free *FYI E-Journal* or access a host of free resources. In addition to hearing your feedback, we'd love for you to contribute a story or idea, or glean a few from other parents like you around the country, at *stickyfaith.org/stories*.

Almost every time I speak to parents about Sticky Faith, I pray that the kids represented by the adults in the room would beat the "one-out-of-two drift-from-the-faith" odds. I ask God to so inspire and equip parents that if we were to fast-forward a number of years, we'd hear story after story of kids who have been changed by Christ to change the world around them. For life.

Our team is praying the same for every reader of this guide — including you and your family.

If you walk away from this guide and make just one change in your family, take just one step forward, we'll consider it a victory. If you listen closely, you'll hear us cheering you on.

The College Transition Project Research Overview

The Fuller Youth Institute's College Transition Project was composed of four separate research initiatives: an initial quantitative pilot study involving sixty-nine youth group graduates; two three-year longitudinal (primarily quantitative) studies of high school seniors during their first three years in college, involving 162 and 227 students respectively; and qualitative interviews with forty-five former youth group graduates between two and four years beyond high school graduation.

In 2004, the Fuller Youth Institute initiated a pilot research study called the College Transition Project (CTP), surveying a group of sixty-nine college students who were alumni of a single youth group in the Northwest. The preliminary results suggested a link between a college student's current spiritual state and the quality of key relationships during the high school years, including the youth group environment itself. As a result, in 2005–6, FYI launched a broader pilot study, recruiting students involved in church youth groups during the spring of their high school senior year. To participate in the survey, students were required to be at least eighteen years of age, be part of a church youth group, and intend to go to a college or university upon graduation. Students were recruited through FYI's nationwide network of youth leader contacts, resulting in a sample of 162 students who were surveyed four times over three years. Thirty of these students participated in subsequent one-hour interviews during their fourth year out of high school.

In 2006–7, enabled by funding from the Lilly Endowment, FYI launched another nationwide longitudinal study of high school seniors connected to church youth groups, to examine their experiences at five points: the spring of their senior year in high school, the fall and spring of their first year in college (2007 and 2008), the spring of their second year in college (2009), and the spring of their third year in college (2010). The primary goal of the study was to determine the programmatic and relational characteristics of families, youth ministries, and churches that have a demonstrable relationship to how students make the adjustment to life beyond high school.

Participants

The sample for this longitudinal study launched in 2007 consisted of 227 high school seniors drawn from different regions across the United States. More than half (56.3 percent) of the respondents were female, while 43.7 percent were male. The sample was predominantly White/ Caucasian (78.0 percent). Asian/Asian American students comprised 11.0 percent of the sample, while Hispanic/Latino students accounted for 5.0 percent. African American and Native American students each accounted for 1.4 percent of the sample. Participants reported a median grade point average of 3.50 to 3.99, with 63 percent of the sample having GPAs above 3.50.[1] The majority of the participants came from larger churches. The median youth group size was 51 – 100 students, while the median church size was reported to be more than 800 members.

Participants were mostly from intact families, with 83.8 percent reporting that they lived with both their father and their mother; another 4.1 percent lived with a parent and stepparent. Overall, the parents of the participants were also well educated. More than two-thirds (69.7 percent) of the mothers held at least a college degree; this figure was nearly three-quarters for the fathers (73.0 percent). By far, the majority of the fathers (88.2 percent) were employed full-time, while fewer than half of the mothers were (42.5 percent).

Procedure

From October 2006 to February 2007, members of the research team who had developed networks in four geographical regions of the United

States (the Southwest, the Northwest, the Southeast, and the Northeast) identified churches representing a diversity of sizes, denominations, socioeconomic levels, and ethnicities. For this study, only churches employing full-time youth pastors were recruited. From March to June 2007, the youth ministry staff of each participating church was asked to invite senior students involved in their youth ministries to participate in the study. As with the pilot, students were eligible only if they were at least eighteen years old and intended to attend a college upon graduation.

Students who agreed to participate in the study could do so in one of three ways: they could complete a paper-and-pencil version of the survey together (facilitated by either their youth pastor or a member of the FYI research team); they could complete a paper version of the survey individually at a time and place convenient for them; or they could complete an online version of the survey. In addition to the survey, each student was required to complete a consent form assuring confidentiality. Signed consent forms also contained an identification code that was unique to each individual, as well as contact information (that is, an email address and a physical address) in order to track each student for future waves of data collection. All future data collection was done via online surveys.

Instruments
Faith Measures

Five measures of faith development were employed in order to create a composite picture of both internalized and externalized faith commitments and behaviors. For four of the measures, participants were asked to rate their agreement with each item on a five-point scale, ranging from "strongly disagree" (1) to "strongly agree" (5). The Intrinsic Religious Motivation Scale[2] is composed of ten items measuring the extent to which an individual's religiosity is not simply external and behavioral but also internalized in terms of one's values and motivations. Sample items include "My faith involves all of my life" and "I try hard to carry my religion over into all my other dealings in life." A similar measure, the Narrative Faith Scale,[3] was developed to assess the extent to which one's decisions are influenced by the sense of having a relationship to God. Sample items include "If and when I date someone, it is (or would be) important to me that God be pleased with the relationship" and "In choosing what college to attend, it is important to me to seek God's will." The third measure is the seventeen-item short form of the Search Institute's Faith Maturity Scale,[4] including items like "My faith shapes how I think and act each and every day" and "My life is committed to Jesus Christ." And the fourth is the God Support Scale,[5] assessing the extent to which participants feel supported and nurtured by God. Using social support items, the scale incorporates indicators such as "I am valued by God."

The fifth measure is a measure of religious behavior created for the CTP pilot. Ten items assess the frequency of engagement in a variety of corporate and individual behaviors, including such items as "pray alone," "read the Bible by yourself," and "attend a worship service or church-related event." Responses are given on a six-point scale, ranging from "less than once a month" (1) to "once a day or more" (6).

Youth Group Experience Measures

Three sets of items were created from qualitative data from earlier stages of the project in order to assess students' participation in and attitudes toward their youth group experience. First, students were asked about the frequency of participation in eight items over the past two months or the past year, including activities like retreats, mission trips, and midweek youth group. Second, participants were presented with twenty-two statements representing why students go to youth group, including "It's where my friends are" and "I learn about God there." Students were asked to rate how true each statement was for them, using a five-point scale ranging from "not true at all" (1) to "completely true" (5). Third, students were asked what they would want to see more or less of in their youth group. Thirteen items were presented, such as "one-on-one time with leaders" and "mission trips." Participants responded on a five-point scale ranging from "much less" (1) to "much more" (5).

Other Measures

In addition to these faith and youth ministry measures, other scales and questions were added related to perceived social support, parental support, support within the youth ministry, loneliness, extraversion, social desirability (as a control factor), and risk behaviors (sexual contact, alcohol use, and pornography use). Subsequent waves of data collection included most of these same measures (particularly faith measures), in addition to scales and questions related to religious behaviors in college, the college spiritual environment, adjustment to college, doubts about faith, parental and other adult contact in college, family faith discussions, preparation for decision making, and college participation in church and campus ministry.

The following are some of the spirituality instruments and their corresponding items.

Intrinsic Religious Motivation Scale

1. My faith involves all of my life.
2. One should seek God's guidance when making every important decision.
3. It doesn't matter so much what I believe as long as I live a moral life.
4. In my life, I experience the presence of the Divine.
5. My faith sometimes restricts my actions.
6. Although I am a religious person, I refuse to let religious considerations influence my everyday affairs.
7. Nothing is as important to me as serving God as best I know how.
8. Although I believe in my religion, I feel there are many more important things in life.
9. I try hard to carry my religion over into all my other dealings in life.
10. My religious beliefs are what really lie behind my whole approach to life.[6]

Narrative Faith Relevance Scale

1. It is important to me that my future career somehow embody a calling from God.

2. I try to see setbacks and crises as part of God's larger plan.

3. If and when I date someone, it is (or would be) important to me that God be pleased with the relationship.

4. In thinking about my schedule, I try to cultivate the attitude that my time belongs to God.

5. It is important to me that whatever money I have be used to serve God's purposes.

6. In choosing what college to attend, it is important to me to seek God's will.

7. When I think of the things I own or would like to own, I try to remember that everything I have belongs to God.[7]

Faith Maturity Scale

1. I experience a deep communion with God.

2. My faith shapes how I think and act each and every day.

3. I help others with their religious questions and struggles.

4. My faith helps me know right from wrong.

5. I devote time to reading and studying the Bible.

6. Every day I see evidence that God is active in the world.

7. I seek out opportunities to help me grow spiritually.

8. I take time for periods of prayer or meditation.

9. I feel God's presence in my relationships with other people.

10. My life is filled with meaning and purpose.

11. I try to apply my faith to political and social issues.

12. My life is committed to Jesus Christ.

13. I go out of my way to show love to people I meet.

14. I have a real sense that God is guiding me.

15. I like to worship and pray with others.

16. I think Christians must be about the business of creating international understanding and harmony.

17. I am spiritually moved by the beauty of God's creation.[8]

Religious Support Scale

1. God gives me the sense that I belong.

2. I feel appreciated by God.

3. If something went wrong, God would give me help.

4. I am valued by God.

5. I can turn to God for advice when I have problems.

6. God cares about my life and situation.

7. I do *not* feel close to God.[9]

High School Version of Religious Behavior Scale (created for the CTP pilot project)

For the following eight items, please tell us how often you engaged in each of the behaviors listed, during *the past twelve months*: Less than once a month, About once a month, Two to three times a month, About once a week, Two to three times a week, Daily.

How often did you:

1. talk with another Christian about your faith, outside of a church-related context?

2. pray alone?

3. attend a worship service or church-related event?

4. speak or try to speak with a non-Christian about your faith?

5. volunteer your time to serve others?

6. participate in a small group of your peers for religious or spiritual purposes?

7. read the Bible by yourself?

8. meet with a spiritual mentor (other than your parents)?

College Version of Religious Behavior Scale

How often did you:

1. talk with another Christian about your faith, outside of a church-related context?

2. participate in an on-campus Christian fellowship?

3. pray alone?

4. attend a worship service or other event at a church off-campus?

5. speak or try to speak with a non-Christian about your faith?

6. volunteer your time to serve others?

7. participate in a small group of your peers for religious or spiritual purposes?

8. read the Bible by yourself?

9. attend a school-sponsored chapel?

10. meet with an older Christian for spiritual growth, mentoring, or discipleship?

11. participate in service or justice work that helps people in need?

The Sticky Faith Families Project Research Overview

The goal of the Fuller Youth Institute's Sticky Faith Families Project was to unearth common practices in the effective transmission of faith from parents to children. Since the subjects in the initial College Transition Project (described in appendix 1) were high school and college students, this subsequent study was designed to complement and flesh out its initial findings through a parent counterpart titled the Sticky Faith Families Project.

Participants

Representatives from FYI contacted fifty-six student ministry pastors from our Sticky Faith Cohort churches and asked them to submit online the names, contact information, and number and ages of children of up to five exemplar parents via SurveyMonkey. The fifty-six nominators were given the following criteria for potential parent participants.

1. The parent has an expressed, ongoing personal relationship with Christ.

2. One or more of their children has an expressed, ongoing personal relationship with Christ.

3. They have incorporated at least one of the following values or activities in their family.

   • Discussions about faith, theology, personal spirituality
   • Involvement in intergenerational community and relationships

- Vacations and holidays geared to build family intimacy and/or faith maturity
- Service projects or activities involving both parents and children
- Integration of grandparents and/or other extended family in the faith development of children

Nominators also included a brief description of why they nominated the parent(s).

Twenty-seven youth pastors responded by nominating a total of eighty-eight sets of parents. Of those eighty-eight sets of parents, forty-one agreed to participate in the study. (Note: While we use the term "set" here, we are referring to either a single- or a double-parent family system. We interviewed some married parents as individuals, some married parents as couples, and some single parents.)

Other demographics of the subjects were as follows:

STATE DISTRIBUTION
California: 14
Wisconsin: 6
Iowa: 4
Minnesota: 4
Michigan: 4
Arkansas: 3
Texas: 2
Idaho: 2
Arizona: 1
Missouri: 1

DENOMINATION
Nondenominational: 12
Presbyterian (PCUSA): 10
Reformed Church of America: 7
Evangelical Free: 4
Nazarene: 3
United Methodist: 3
Church of Christ: 1
Lutheran: 1

Methodology

The research method was a semistructured interview format. Subjects participated in sixty-minute to seventy-five-minute phone interviews with a research team member. The interview proper consisted of nine questions, with follow-up questions asked as appropriate for clarification or elaboration.

The primary questions used for the interviews were:

1. In the midst of any busy seasons your family has experienced, how have you tried to stay connected with your children?

2. When have you tended to have your best conversations about faith with your children? Why do you think those conversations went well?

3. What, if any, impact have intergenerational relationships (that is, your child being connected to other adults) made in your child's life and spiritual development?

4. What, if anything, have you done to try to make your vacations or extended time away with your children meaningful for your family?

5. In what ways have you tried to structure your home environment so that it was a nurturing space for your family's faith development?

6. In what ways have you tried to instill in your children a heart for those who are poor or engage in service together as a family?

7. Looking back, what do you wish you had done differently when it comes to instilling or sharing your faith with your children?

8. What advice would you want to share with parents of young children? Are there particular events or experiences in your own parenting that motivate you to share that advice? If so, would you be open to sharing those?

9. What advice would you want to share with parents of adolescents? Are there particular events or experiences in your own parenting that motivate you to share that advice? If so, would you be willing to share them?

These interviews were scheduled and took place (forty on the phone, one in person) in July, August, and early September of 2012. Four trained interviewers conducted the interviews, including Dr. Kara Powell. The responses were recorded and were subsequently transcribed. Each transcription was reviewed for accuracy by the respective interviewer.

Data Analysis

The interview team met at the completion of the interviews and transcription. Questions and general themes were discussed among team members. Following this meeting, each team member individually coded three interviews, and at a subsequent meeting, the team corroborated primary and secondary themes for ongoing coding by two team members. These two researchers then coded all of the interviews, beginning again with three transcripts, discussing their coding for consistency, and moving forward through the interview corpus. The entire team reviewed the coding following this process, identifying emerging trends, clustered themes, and cross-domain themes. From this work, additional research literature was consulted prior to meetings with focus groups to discuss preliminary findings.

Following this process, focus groups were held with leaders gathered at two Sticky Faith Cohort summits in February 2013. General themes and insights were shared, along with a set of questions geared to elicit insights, observations, and further questions. Leaders in the focus groups spoke both from the perspective of their work with parents in ministry as well as from their experiences as parents (for those who were also parents).

Subsequent Interviews and Focus Groups

Given the input received in the February 2013 focus groups, the same research team that completed the first forty-one interviews collected more data. An additional focus group was conducted with single parents in March 2013 in order to gain insight from that particular subgroup on the initial findings. In May and June 2013, nine additional interviews were conducted by Dr. Kara Powell with parents known through the networks of the Fuller Youth Institute. Special attention was given to selecting interview subjects who not only fit the initial nomination criteria but also could help answer questions raised in the February 2013 focus groups or who could help bring more racial, ethnic, and socioeconomic diversity to the pool of participants, since the initial round of interviews didn't yield the desired diverse representation.

In addition to answering some of the previous nine interview questions, respondents were asked to respond to a portion of these additional questions:

1. In the midst of your own busyness, how have you tried to develop your own relationship with God? In other words, how have you "tended your own flame"?

2. What specifically have you done to strengthen your marriage in the midst of parenting?

3. Often parents are aware of what they do wrong and the mistakes they make. How have you tried to forgive yourself for your parenting mistakes and flaws?

4. How do you try to show your kids grace when they blow it?

5. What have you done to try to control your anger toward your kids?

6. What practices or habits in your family helped you develop a closer relationship with your kid when he or she was in preschool or elementary school?

7. What practices or habits in your family helped you develop a closer relationship with your kid when he or she was in middle school or high school?

8. How did you try to get involved in your teenager's world (meaning their hobbies, friendships, and school or extracurricular experiences)?

9. As a mom, what did you do to try to build your relationship with your child?

10. As a dad, what did you do to try to build your relationship with your child?

11. What did you do to try to prepare your graduating high school senior for what they would face after graduation? (This preparation could be spiritual, relational, or logistical.)

12. What did you do to make your home and family a safe place to talk about your child's tough questions, struggles, and even doubts?

13. What happened in your family that helped your child really own their own faith?

14. What else do you think I would want to know about who your family is or what your family does?

Notes

Chapter 1: Why Does Your Family Need a Sticky Faith Guide?

1. A 2011 study of young adults indicates that approximately 59 percent of young people with a Christian background report that they have dropped out of church (David Kinnaman and Aly Hawkins, *You Lost Me* [Grand Rapids, Mich.: Baker, 2011]).

   According to a Gallup Poll, approximately 40 percent of eighteen- to twenty-nine-year-olds who attended church when they were sixteen or seventeen years old are no longer attending (George H. Gallup Jr., "The Religiosity Cycle," *Gallup Poll*, October 19, 2006; Frank Newport, "A Look at Religious Switching in America Today," *Gallup Poll*, 2006, October 19, 2006).

   A 2007 survey by LifeWay Research of more than one thousand adults ages eighteen to thirty who spent a year or more in youth group during high school suggests that more than 65 percent of young adults who attend a Protestant church for at least a year in high school will stop attending church regularly for at least a year between the ages of eighteen and twenty-two. In this study, respondents were not necessarily seniors who had graduated from youth group. In addition, the research design did not factor in parachurch or on-campus faith communities in their definition of college "church" attendance.

   Data from the National Study of Youth and Religion published in 2009 indicates approximately a 30 percent drop in frequent religious service attendance across multiple Protestant denominations (Christian Smith with Patricia Snell, *Souls in Transition: The Religious and Spiritual Lives of Emerging Adults* [New York: Oxford Univ. Press, 2009]).

   FYI's estimate that 40–50 percent of high school graduates will fail to stick with their faith is based on a compilation of data from these various studies.

2. When we use the phrase "fall away from the faith," we don't necessarily mean that students have lost their salvation, but rather we mean that they have fallen away from a faith that places Jesus at the center of all they are and do.

3. All names, and at times a few additional details, have been changed to preserve the privacy of the people we interviewed. These changes are minor and do not affect the essence of the parents' ideas or experiences.

4. Approximately 15 percent of the ideas in this book come from additional parents our team met during the course of our research. While not officially included in the fifty we interviewed, in general these parents fit most, if not all, of the criteria used to select those fifty parents.

Chapter 2: **You Get What You Are**

1. Christian Smith and Melissa Lundquist Denton, *Soul Searching* (New York: Oxford Univ. Press, 2005), 57. The importance of parental example is confirmed in a number of studies, including Pam E. King and Ross A. Mueller, "Parental Influence on Adolescent Religiousness: Exploring the Roles of Spiritual Modeling and Social Capital," *Marriage and Family: A Christian Journal* 6, no. 3 (2003): 401–13.

2. W. N. Bao, D. H. Whitbeck, D. Hoyt, and R. C. Conger, "Perceived Parental Acceptance as a Moderator of Religious Transmission among Adolescent Boys and Girls," *Journal of Marriage and the Family* 61 (1999): 362–74. L. Okagaki and C. Bevis, "Transmission of Religious Values: Relations between Parents' and Daughters' Beliefs," *Journal of Genetic Psychology* 160 (1999): 303–18.

3. Paul R. Amato and Alan Booth, *A Generation at Risk: Growing Up in an Era of Family Upheaval* (Cambridge: Harvard Univ. Press, 1997), 139–42.

4. To take a free profile to identify your love language, visit *5lovelanguages.com*.

Chapter 3: **Handling Mistakes**

1. Dallas Willard, *The Divine Conspiracy* (San Francisco: HarperCollins, 1998), 41.

2. Dietrich Bonhoeffer, *The Cost of Discipleship* (New York: Macmillan, 1963), 47.

Chapter 4: **Warm Family Relationships**

1. Vern L. Bengtson, Norella M. Putney, and Susan Harris, *Families and Faith* (New York: Oxford Univ. Press, 2013). This finding has been confirmed by multiple studies across a variety of faith traditions over the past three decades.

2. Ibid., 76–79.

3. Ibid., 74–76.

Chapter 5: **Connecting**

1. This is also a theme in Chap Clark, *Hurt 2.0: Inside the World of Today's Teenagers* (Grand Rapids, Mich.: Baker, 2011).

2. The Search Institute, *Insights and Evidence: Finding the Student Spark* 5, no. 1 (November 2010).

3. Reggie Joiner and Carey Nieuwhof, *Parenting beyond Your Capacity* (Colorado Springs: David C. Cook, 2010), 135.

4. Richard A. Swenson, *Margin* (Colorado Springs: NavPress, 1992), 91–92.

5. Vern L. Bengtson, Norella M. Putney, and Susan Harris, *Families and Faith* (New York: Oxford Univ. Press, 2013), 229–30.

Chapter 6: Community

1. Elizabeth Marquardt, *Between Two Worlds: The Inner Lives of Children of Divorce* (New York: Crown, 2005).

2. *Developmental Assets: A Profile of Your Youth* (Minneapolis: Search Institute, 2005), unpublished report.

3. Scott McConnell, "LifeWay Research Finds Reasons 18- to 22-Year-Olds Drop out of Church" (August 7, 2007), *lifeway.com/Article/LifeWay-Research-finds-reasons-18-to-22-year-olds-drop-out-of-church*.

4. Robert D. Putnam, *Bowling Alone: The Collapse and Revival of American Community* (New York: Simon & Schuster, 2000), 299.

5. William Damon, *The Youth Charter* (New York: Free Press, 1997), 62.

Chapter 7: Grandparents and Senior Adults

1. Adapted from the definition of "functional family" in Diana R. Garland, *Family Ministry* (Downers Grove, Ill.: InterVarsity, 1999), 38.

2. Vern L. Bengtson, Norella M. Putney, and Susan Harris, *Families and Faith* (New York: Oxford Univ. Press, 2013), 100.

3. Ibid., 104–12.

4. Ibid., 101–4.

5. V. King and G. H. Elder Jr., "Are Religious Grandparents More Involved Grandparents?" *Journal of Gerontology: Social Sciences* 54: S317–28.

Chapter 8: Communication

1. Walter Isaacson, *Steve Jobs* (New York: Simon & Schuster, 2011), 14–15.

2. *Developmental Assets: A Profile of Your Youth* (Minneapolis: Search Institute, 2005), 2003 weighted aggregate dataset, unpublished report.

3. Those two datasets are the National Study of Youth and Religion and the National Longitudinal Study of Adolescent Health (Mark D. Regnerus, *Forbidden Fruit* [New York: Oxford Univ. Press, 2007], 60–73).

4. D. C. Dollahite and J. Y. Thatcher, "Talking about Religion: How Religious Youth and Parents Discuss Their Faith," *Journal of Adolescent Research* 23 (2008): 611–41.

5. A. Desrosiers, B. S. Kelly, and L. Miller, "Parent and Peer Relationships and Relational Spirituality in Adolescents and Young Adults," *Psychology of Religion and Spirituality* 3 (2011): 39–54.

Chapter 10: Home Sticky Home

1. Pew Research Center, *Pew Internet and American Life Project* (June 28, 2012), *http://pewinternet.org/Infographics/2012/A-Closer-Look-at-Gadget-Ownership.aspx*.

2. Pew Research Center, *Pew Internet and American Life Project* (July 11, 2011), *http://pewinternet.org/Infographics/2011/Smartphones.aspx*.

3. Pew Research Center, *Pew Internet and American Life Project* (August 5, 2013), *http:// pewinternet.org/Commentary/2012/March/Pew-Internet-Social-Networking-full-detail .aspx.*

4. Pew Research Center, *Pew Internet and American Life Project* (October 19, 2008), *http://pew internet.org/Reports/2008/Networked-Families.aspx.*

5. Bradley Howell, "Using Social Media to Strengthen Family Bonds," *FYI E-Journal* (July 8, 2013), *http://fulleryouthinstitute.org/articles/using-social-media-to-strengthen-family-bonds.*

6. Kelly Musick and Ann Meier, "Assessing Causality and Persistence in Associations between Family Dinners and Adolescent Well-Being," *Journal of Marriage and Family* 74 (June 2012): 476 – 93.

Chapter 11: **Service That Sticks**

1. By justice, we mean the restoration of God's *shalom*, which includes peace with God, with other humans, with nature, and with oneself. One simple way we often describe this restoration to teenagers is as the "righting of wrongs." See Chap Clark and Kara E. Powell, *Deep Justice in a Broken World* (Grand Rapids, Mich.: Zondervan, 2007).

2. Kurt Ver Beek, "The Impact of Short-Term Missions: A Case Study of House Construction in Honduras after Hurricane Mitch," *Missiology* 34, no. 4 (October 2006): 485.

3. Robert J. Priest, Terry Dischinger, Steve Rasmussen, and C. M. Brown, "Researching the Short-Term Mission Movement," *Missiology* 34, no. 4 (October 2006): 431 – 50.

4. The following section is adapted from an article by Kara Powell, Dave Livermore, Terry Linhart, and Brad Griffin titled "If We Send Them, They Will Grow ... Maybe," available at *fulleryouthinstitute.org.*

5. This model was originally proposed by Laura Joplin and later modified and tested by Dr. Terry Linhart on youth mission trips. See Laura Joplin, "On Defining Experiential Education," in K. Warren, M. Sakofs, and J. S. Hunt Jr., eds., *The Theory of Experiential Education* (Dubuque, Iowa: Kendall/Hunt, 1995), 15 – 22, and Terrence D. Linhart, "Planting Seeds: The Curricular Hope of Short-Term Mission Experiences in Youth Ministry," *Christian Education Journal* series 3 (2005): 256 – 72. Some of the terminology in the model has been modified.

6. This model is fully explained in Kara Powell and Brad Griffin, *Deep Justice Journeys* (Grand Rapids, Mich.: Zondervan, 2009), which provides fifty before/during/after learning activities to help teenagers move from mission trips to missional living.

7. Diana Garland, *Inside Out Families* (Waco, Texas: Baylor Univ. Press, 2010), 69.

Chapter 12: **Sticky Transitions**

1. The phrase "emerging adult" was coined by Jeffrey J. Arnett in 2001 and has gained great acceptance since then. Arnett used the term to include roughly the ages eighteen to twenty-five and believes that this age group is characterized by iden-

tity exploration, instability, self-focus, feeling in between, and believing in great possibilities. See Jeffrey J. Arnett, *Adolescence and Emerging Adulthood* (New Jersey: Prentice Hall, 2001), 8.

2. Michael D. Berzonsky et al., "Parental Psychological Control and Dimensions of Identity Formation in Emerging Adulthood," *Journal of Family Psychology* 21, no. 3 (2007): 546–50.

3. Hara Estroff Marano, *A Nation of Wimps: The High Cost of Invasive Parenting* (New York: Random House, 2008), 31. For more on the effects of helicopter parenting, see Stephenie Lievense, "The Proper Care and Feeding of Emerging Adults: Parenting Strategies for Launching Kids into Adulthood" (two parts), *FYI E-Journal*, *http://fulleryouthinstitute.org/articles/the-proper-care-and-feeding-of-emerging-adults#fn-7-a* and *http://fulleryouthinstitute.org/articles/the-proper-care-and-feeding-of-emerging-adults2*.

4. Tim Clydesdale, *The First Year Out* (Chicago: Univ. of Chicago Press, 2007).

Appendix 1: The College Transition Project Research Overview

1. This is higher than the average GPA for college-bound seniors nationwide, which was reported in 2006 as 3.28 ("Nation's Report Card," 2006).

2. D. R. Hoge, "A Validated Intrinsic Religious Motivation Scale," *Journal for the Scientific Study of Religion* 11 (1972): 369–76.

3. Cameron Lee, "Narrative Faith Relevance Scale" (2004), unpublished manuscript.

4. P. L. Benson, M. J. Donahue, and J. A. Erickson, "The Faith Maturity Scale: Conceptualization, Measurement, and Empirical Validation," *Research in the Social Scientific Study of Religion* 5 (1993): 1–26.

5. William E. Fiala, Jeffrey P. Bjorck, and Richard Gorsuch, "The Religious Support Scale: Construction, Validation, and Cross-Validation," *American Journal of Community Psychology* 30 (2002): 761–86.

6. Hoge, "Validated Intrinsic Religious Motivation Scale."

7. Lee, "Narrative Faith Relevance Scale."

8. Benson et al., "Faith Maturity Scale."

9. Fiala et al., "Religious Support Scale."

Sticky Faith

Everyday Ideas to Build Lasting Faith in Your Kids

Dr. Kara E. Powell
and Dr. Chap Clark

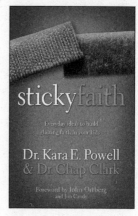

Nearly every Christian parent in America would give anything to find a viable resource for developing within their kids a deep, dynamic faith that "sticks" long term. *Sticky Faith* delivers. Research shows that almost half of graduating high school seniors struggle deeply with their faith. Recognizing the ramifications of that statistic, the Fuller Youth Institute (FYI) conducted the College Transition Project in an effort to identify the relationships and best practices that can set young people on a trajectory of lifelong faith and service. Based on FYI findings, this easy-to-read guide presents both a compelling rationale and a powerful strategy to show parents how to encourage their children's spiritual growth so that it will stick to them into adulthood and empower them to develop a living, lasting faith. Written by authors known for the integrity of their research and the intensity of their passion for young people, *Sticky Faith* is geared to spark a movement that empowers adults to develop robust and long-term faith in kids of all ages.

Available in stores and online!